YOUR GRIDIRON GOURMET

A COLLECTION OF RECIPES CELEBRATING
FOOD, FAMILY, FRIENDS, AND FOOTBALL

Lisa Jensen

Photography by Michelle Fish of FishEye Photography

YOUR GRIDIRON GOURMET

A COLLECTION OF RECIPES CELEBRATING FOOD, FAMILY, FRIENDS, AND FOOTBALL

Copyright © 2011 by
J and A Associates, LLC
4639 E. Mountainview Court
Phoenix, Arizona 85028
www.yourgridirongourmet.com

Photography © by Michelle Fish/FishEye Photography except as noted below
Photography pages 52, 64, 67, 68, 84, and 100 © by Lisa Jensen
Photography page 116 © by Jacquelin Rognehaugh

Published by

 Favorite Recipes® Press

An imprint of

 INC

A wholly owned subsidiary of Southwestern
P.O. Box 305142
Nashville, Tennessee 37230
800-358-0560

Editorial Director: Mary Cummings
Book Design: Steve Newman
Project Editor: Cathy Ropp

ISBN: 978-0-615-46230-1

This cookbook is a collection of favorite recipes,
which are not necessarily original recipes.

Manufactured in China
First Printing: 2011   3,000 copies

INTRODUCTION

Every football season, my husband and I get out a long list. Not a list of our favorite teams, rituals, side bets, or games we want to see. We pull out a messy handwritten compilation of our favorite foods to make while celebrating and watching American football. Every year the list just kept getting longer, and every year we fumbled our way through trying to find and then trying to read our scribbled notes and recipes. When we finally decided to tackle putting everything down on paper, we came up with some really fun recipe names, created a signature recipe for each pro football team, and much more. As you might guess, the makings of a cookbook evolved faster than a running back doing 40 yards in 4.4! This is not our first cookbook, and hopefully not our last, but this cookbook truly comes from our hearts. It has given us the opportunity to not only share our absolute favorite recipes, but also to share our love of food, family, friends, and football.

This book is dedicated to my husband, Mark Armstrong, for being instigator, football commentator, recipe critic, and the *life* in our lives.

TABLE OF CONTENTS

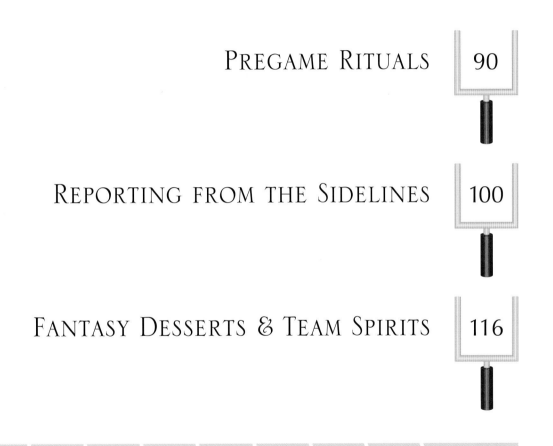

ARIZONA SPICED BEEF BRISKET CHILI

SLOW-COOKIN' SUNDAYS

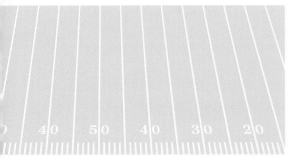

In the Sunday section of our cookbook, we feature dishes that are fun to make for a crowd, or better yet *with* a crowd, as these recipes are tailored to get everyone in the game while watching the game! In these recipes, after the initial preparation, the food does all the work by either slow cooking on top of the stove or in the oven. That way, everyone can sit back, relax, and watch a favorite pro team pass, kick, and tackle. In this section we teach you how to be a real Gridiron Gourmet! We look after the X's and O's and relieve your game-day jitters by offering prep tips with easy play-by-play recipe instructions for the meals that might make most rookies turn and run to the locker room.

Are you ready for some FOOTBALL?? . . . Well, football food that is.

Arizona Spiced Beef Brisket Chili

Serves 8 (or 4 linebackers!)

We start off our cookbook with an amazing rendition of undeniably the most popular football food of all: a super-hearty, super-satisfying, Super Bowl-worthy take on the football classic: CHILI.

Leave hamburger on the sidelines! Get your football arm in shape by slicing up a whole beef brisket into bite-size cubes and then chopping up some butternut squash (not an easy veggie to tackle) as the key ingredients to this mouthwatering meaty main course!

Butternut squash in chili?? Yes! We have been making chili with beef brisket for years, but upon eyeing a recipe with butternut squash on the cover of a food magazine, we had to try it. The squash adds wonderful color, smoothness, and a touch of sweetness making the chili something that just could . . . go . . . all . . . the way!

Prep Coach

1   To slice the beef brisket, cut it across the grain into 1-inch strips. Cut the fat off the bottom of each slice, if desired. Then, cut each strip into 1-inch cubes. Place beef in a large bowl and generously season with 2 teaspoons salt and 1 teaspoon pepper. Allow beef to sit while you are preparing everything else.

2   To chop the butternut squash, don't peel it first because it becomes very slippery as you remove the layer of skin. Cut it into 1-inch-thick rounds (be careful, as this type of squash can be hard to cut through), then lay each round flat on the cutting board and chop off the skin in small pieces. Then, chop the squash into 1-inch cubes. The thicker part of the squash may have seeds that need to be removed.

3   Get creative with the chili powder. Don't use the same old chili powder that has been sitting on your spice rack for years. Use chipotle chili powder (hot), New Mexican chili powder (medium), ancho chili powder (mild), or cayenne (hot), which also work well. Or, make it your own dish by creating a special mix of chili powders and, of course, tell your friends that they can't buy it off you for love or money. Well, maybe for a Super Bowl ticket or two.

4   Chili can be made a day ahead, and in fact, the brisket further tenderizes overnight. If you do this, take chili from the refrigerator and allow it to come to room temperature. Reheat on your stovetop over medium heat, stirring occasionally.

5   Set out the garnishes just before serving so guests can pick and choose their toppings.

You will need a large ovenproof pot because this chili is not going to sit on top of the stove and simmer slowly! We are going to put it in the oven and bake it at 350 degrees for 4 hours so the brisket melts in your mouth when you take that first beefy bite.

Ingredients

1   tablespoon vegetable oil
2   large onions, chopped
3   large celery stalks, chopped
1   jalapeño pepper, cut in half lengthwise, seeds and membrane removed, then minced
1   (3- to 4-pound) whole flat-cut beef brisket, prepared using the PREP COACH
2   (14-ounce) cans diced tomatoes with juices
2   (4-ounce) cans diced roasted green chilies
1   (15-ounce) can red kidney beans, drained and rinsed
1   (15-ounce) can pinto beans, drained and rinsed
1   cup beef broth
1   (12-ounce) bottle Mexican beer
1   teaspoon cumin
8   shakes of your favorite hot sauce, such as Tabasco
1 or 2 tablespoons chili powder (If you are using a hotter variety, 1 tablespoon will be enough)
3   cups butternut squash, peeled and cut in 1-inch pieces (keep refrigerated as it will be added during the last hour of cooking)

Preparation

Preheat oven to 350 degrees.

Heat oil in a large ovenproof pot (an 8-quart stockpot works best) over medium heat.

Add onions and celery and sauté until soft—about 8 to 10 minutes.

Add jalapeño and sauté another minute.

Add beef to pot (no need to brown the meat).

Add tomatoes, chilies, beans, broth, beer, cumin and hot sauce.

Continue to cook over medium heat, stirring constantly.

Add chili powder or your mix of chili powders per our PREP COACH suggestions. This may be too spicy for some, so use less if you are not accustomed to spice or if you choose to use the hotter varieties of chilies!

More spice can be added later after a taste test; mix well.

Keep the pot at medium heat and bring chili to a simmer, stirring frequently.

Cover and place in the oven. Bake for 3 hours.

After 3 hours, remove chili from the oven and stir in the squash.

Before putting chili back in the oven, do a taste test and add more chili powder, hot sauce, salt or pepper, if desired. Add liquid at this point (as in more beer!) if chili is too dry. Place pot back into oven. Bake, covered, for 1 more hour.

Place your choice of garnishes in separate bowls to serve with the chili.

Garnishes

Fresh cilantro
Shredded Cheddar cheese
Sour cream
Celery sticks
Tortilla chips

Marilyn's Cincinnati Chili

Serves 6

Cincinnati Chili is a specially seasoned ground beef mixture that when slow cooked turns almost into a paste. It is served over spaghetti along with toppings served "2 to 5 ways."

2-Way is spaghetti and chili.
3-Way is spaghetti, chili, and cheese.
4-Way is spaghetti, chili, cheese, and onions.
5-Way is spaghetti, chili, cheese, onions, and beans.
All-Way is with everything plus oyster crackers!

The recipe most certainly originated from Greek immigrants. Some say it was invented by Tom and John Kiradjieff way back in 1922 when they served it over hot dogs and spaghetti at their small hot dog stand. But don't tell that to the Skyline Chili creator Nicholas Lambrinides, also from Greece, whose first restaurant overlooked the Cincinnati skyline in 1949.

Prep Coach

1 Break up the ground beef well with your hands while adding it to the pot of water.

2 Stir well every 30 minutes or so to ensure the mixture ends up resembling a paste.

Ingredients

2 quarts (8 cups) water
2 pounds uncooked ground beef (not lean)
2 tablespoons regular mild chili powder
1 tablespoon salt
1 teaspoon cinnamon
1 teaspoon black pepper
1 teaspoon allspice
1 teaspoon Worcestershire sauce
1/2 teaspoon cumin
1/2 teaspoon red pepper flakes
3 bay leaves
1 (6-ounce) can tomato paste
2 tablespoons cider vinegar
2 garlic cloves, minced
2 cups diced onion
1 pound uncooked thin spaghetti

Garnishes

1 (15-ounce) can kidney beans
3 cups shredded Cheddar cheese (or more)
1 cup finely chopped fresh onion
Oyster crackers

Everyone from Ohio will love this version of the famous Cincinnati chili given to us by Marilyn Attinger!

PREPARATION

Add the 2 quarts water to a large stockpot.

Add the ground beef, breaking it up with your hands while adding it to the pot.

Bring water and beef to a boil, reduce to simmer and simmer for 30 minutes, stirring occasionally to ensure beef cooks into very fine crumbles.

Add remaining ingredients except for the spaghetti and the garnishes.

Bring to a boil, reduce to simmer and simmer 4 hours with no lid (do not cover), stirring every 30 minutes or so. The chili is done when it has cooked down to resemble a paste and all liquid has been cooked away.

Rinse the kidney beans, place in a small pot and bring to a boil. Reduce heat to medium and simmer the beans for 5 minutes.

Cook pasta according to package directions and then drain well.

PLATING

Place the beans, shredded Cheddar cheese, onion and oyster crackers into individual serving bowls.

Divide the pasta among 6 plates, spoon some of the chili over each and add garnishes as desired.

COLORADO FIRE-ZONE BLITZ CHILE VERDE

Serves 6 to 8

A fire-zone blitz is a great invention of some of the most devious defensive football minds in the game today. It involves sending multiple personnel from the same side or area of the defense after the opposing quarterback and dropping others to cover their places. This overloads the pass protection and can be a real source of indigestion for the center and quarterback trying to coordinate the pass blocking.

In the case of this recipe, be prepared to burn, sting, cough, and certainly cry! You thought onions were bad. Cutting into even mild fresh chilies can make you feel as if you have been pepper sprayed, but roasting your own chilies is fun! Canned fire-roasted green chilies can, of course, be used for this recipe, but have a look at the PREP COACH below for how to roast your own.

This recipe calls for green chilies, which are not the green bell peppers you use in every day cooking; don't confuse the two. Look for New Mexico Hatch or Anaheim green chilies in the vegetable section of your local grocer. Hatch chilies are seasonal, so you might have better luck finding the Anaheim variety. Do not use just any green chilies; jalapeños would be far too hot for this recipe, for example. Do not substitute dried chilies for fresh.

This wonderful chili verde (green chili sauce) is made with either pork or beef sirloin that has slow cooked until the meat breaks down to sublime tenderness. Serve it inside tortillas with numerous garnishes that guests can pile on in whatever order they choose.

INGREDIENTS

2 pounds pork loin chops or beef sirloin steaks, cubed in 1-inch pieces

Mixture of $1/2$ cup flour, 1 teaspoon salt, $1/2$ teaspoon pepper and $1/2$ teaspoon cumin

3 tablespoons vegetable oil

1 large onion, chopped

3 large celery stalks, diced

4 fresh garlic cloves, minced

1 (12-ounce) bottle Mexican beer (can substitute beer with beef broth)

8 fresh Hatch or Anaheim chilies prepared per PREP COACH, or two 4-ounce cans diced fire-roasted green chilies

$2 1/2$ cups beef broth

Salt and pepper

$1/3$ cup chopped fresh cilantro

Large (10-inch) flour tortillas— 1 or 2 per person

PREP COACH

1 To prepare the chilies, cut off tops of chilies and half each lengthwise. Remove seeds and membranes from inside chilies by running cool water over them. Remember to wear gloves when handling hot chilies. Place skin side up on a large baking sheet, pressing down to flatten. Roast chilies under highest position of a broiler and broil until skins are blackened. Allow to cool 15 minutes. Peel the skin off the chilies (don't worry if some of the skin does not peel off completely), discard skins, finely chop chilies and set aside. Don't rub your eyes for 12 hours!

Eight chilies yield about 1 cup chopped roasted chilies. Can be made ahead up to 3 days. Freeze for up to 6 months.

2 If you cannot find fresh chilies, use two 4-ounce cans (1 cup) diced fired-roasted green chilies.

In certain parts of the country, such as in Colorado and New Mexico, you can purchase fresh or preroasted Hatch chilies at roadside stands during the fall.

PREPARATION

Combine cubed pork or beef with flour mixture and stir to coat.

In a large stockpot, heat 2 tablespoons oil over medium-high heat.

Add the pork or beef along with any residual flour and sauté until well browned on all sides, about 8 to 10 minutes.

Remove meat from pot, place in a bowl and set aside.

In same pot, add 1 tablespoon oil, onion and celery and cook until tender, about 6 minutes. Add garlic and sauté another minute.

Add the beer and stir to deglaze the pot for 1 minute, scraping up and saving the browned bits in the pot.

Add the chilies and the browned pork or beef and stir well. Stir in the beef broth, stir, and bring to a boil. Reduce the heat to low and simmer, covered, stirring occasionally, for 2 hours.

After 2 hours do a taste test and add salt and pepper to taste.

Simmer 1 more hour. The chili should have the appearance of a thick stew. If the chili needs to thicken, increase heat to a low boil and simmer with the lid off for the remaining 30 minutes.

Stir in fresh cilantro just before serving.

PLATING

Place 1 tortilla on each plate. Using a ladle, pour a ladleful of chili verde down the middle of each tortilla. Fold or roll up seam side down. Add another couple tablespoons of chili verde over each tortilla. Add garnishes.

GARNISHES

Sour cream
Salsa or chopped fresh tomatoes
Shredded Cheddar or Mexican cheese
Shredded lettuce
Diced avocado or prepared guacamole

PAULA G'S SHORT RIBS

Serves 6

These are much better than bruised ribs for sure. Ask any running back by about Week 12 of the season!

Beef short ribs are usually slow cooked with liquid (braised) rather than smoked or grilled, and are quite fatty, but also quite meaty. When asking for them from your local grocer, they can be cut into 2-inch pieces (English cut) or into 1/2-inch pieces (flanken cut). Another popular cut, though not suitable for this recipe, is the Korean style, where they are butterflied into long strips and grilled. My sister's recipe offers a slow-cooked method of braising the meat in the oven until tender as can be. We suggest that you serve them on top of our Creamy Mashed Potatoes on page 113.

PREP COACH

1   This recipe calls for 4 pounds of bone-in short ribs, which yields about 12 pieces. If you are feeding less than six, simply purchase 2 pieces per person. Four pounds sounds like a lot, but due to the bone-in and fat content, they cook down quite a bit. Your local grocer can assist you with the proper amount to purchase. It is important to trim the ribs of all exterior fat before browning.

2   The garlic, onion, carrots and celery will be discarded so the size you chop them into is not all that important—1/2-inch pieces or so would be fine.

3   When retrieving the ribs from the pot after braising, the meat will most likely have fallen off the bone. You may need to search around a bit with a slotted spoon to obtain all the pieces.

4   Start the Mashed Potatoes after 2 1/2 hours of braising; rewarm if needed.

These short ribs are covered with a rich, dark beer and then braised in the oven.

INGREDIENTS

1   cup flour
1   teaspoon salt
1   teaspoon pepper
4   pounds bone-in beef short ribs, trimmed of exterior fat
2   tablespoons olive oil
4   garlic cloves, smashed, skins removed and cloves left whole
1   onion, coarsely chopped
3   carrots, peeled and coarsely chopped
3   celery stalks, coarsely chopped
1/2   teaspoon dried rosemary
2   (14-ounce) cans beef broth
1   bottle dark beer, such as Guinness Stout

PREPARATION

Preheat oven to 275 degrees.
Add flour to a large bowl and stir in salt and pepper. In batches, dredge ribs in flour on all sides.
Heat the oil in a large ovenproof pot (such as a 6- or 8-quart stockpot) over medium heat and add short ribs with tongs in batches to brown on all sides, about 8 minutes per batch, adding more oil if necessary.
Transfer browned short ribs to a platter.

(continued on next page)

Add garlic cloves, onion, carrots and
celery to the same pot and sauté
until browned, about 6 minutes.
Add beef broth to same pot
and stir to deglaze the pot for
1 minute, scraping up and saving
the browned bits in the pot.

Add the dark beer and stir.

Add browned ribs, pushing them
into the broth (some may not be
completely covered).

Bring pot to a boil, cover with a
lid and place in the oven.

Braise for 3 hours.

When ribs are done, carefully transfer
with tongs to a platter. Some of
the rib meat may have fallen off
the bone so you may need to
search around a bit with a slotted
spoon to obtain all the pieces.
Cover ribs with foil to keep warm.

Pour cooking liquid through a
strainer over a saucepan and
discard solids.

Optional: If you wish to thicken the juices,
remove about 2/3 cup of the juices
from the saucepan and cool in a small
bowl. Add 3 tablespoons flour and
whisk until incorporated. Add the
flour mixture to the remaining juices
in the saucepan and whisk again until
smooth. Bring sauce to a boil to thicken.

Simmer juices or sauce until ready
to serve.

Place a mound of mashed potatoes
on each of 6 plates.

Top with rib meat and spoon some
of the juices or the sauce over
the ribs.

SERVE WITH

Refreshing Cucumber Salad
(page 105)
Creamy Mashed Potatoes (page 113)

BEEF BRISKET FRENCH DIPS

Serves 6

Nothing slow cooks better, easier, and comes out more tender than a beef brisket. When sliced warm and placed on toasted rolls with a bit of horseradish mayonnaise and dipped in the cooking juices, it will certainly become one of your favorite football sandwich meals. We like to serve this dish with our Potato Salad with Bits of Bacon on page 105.

Our beef brisket is first smothered in caramelized onions and then braised in beef broth and garlic cloves for 3 hours.

PREP COACH

1 Make sure you have a baking dish large enough to hold the brisket. If you purchase a medium-size brisket, it should easily fit into a standard 9×13-inch baking dish.

2 Cook the onions on medium heat. You want them to brown and caramelize, not burn.

INGREDIENTS

2   tablespoons butter
3   large onions, sliced into thin rings
1   whole beef brisket of medium size (3 to 4 pounds)
1 to 2 (14-ounce) cans of beef broth
1/2 teaspoon salt
1/2 teaspoon red pepper flakes
6   whole garlic cloves
1/3 cup mayonnaise
1   teaspoon creamy horseradish
6   hoagie rolls, French rolls or other favorite rolls

PREPARATION

Preheat oven to 300 degrees.

In a large skillet, melt butter over medium heat. Add onions and sauté for 20 minutes.

It is easiest to use a pair of tongs to flip the onions as they cook. You want the onions to have a nice caramel color, so turn down the heat if onions start to become too dark.

After 10 minutes, the onions should start to lightly brown. Continue sautéing for a total of 20 minutes or even longer if necessary.

Place brisket fat side down in a 9×13-inch baking dish or other dish that allows it to lay flat.

Pour enough beef broth over the brisket to cover it half way (about 1 cup).

Sprinkle salt and red pepper flakes over the brisket.

With cooking tongs, evenly lay the onions over the brisket.

Place the whole garlic cloves in the baking dish, 3 on each side.

Cover tightly with foil and cook in the oven for 3 hours.

Mix the mayonnaise and horseradish in a small bowl and keep refrigerated.

Remove brisket from the oven and be sure to reserve pan juices.

Transfer brisket to a cutting board and let rest 5 to 10 minutes.

Pour pan juices into a medium saucepan and keep warm over low heat. Discard garlic.

Add a can of beef broth to the pan juices if the juice looks too thin or if there is not enough, as you will need to divide the pan juices for dipping. Set oven to broil.

While brisket is resting, cut hoagie rolls in half and place cut side up on a baking sheet.

Broil rolls on the center rack of open oven for a few seconds until toasted.

Remove rolls to cool.

Slice brisket into thin slices. Cut away and discard the bottom layer of fat.

Divide the pan juices among 6 cups for dipping.

Spread desired amount of horseradish mayonnaise on each roll and top with slices of brisket and onion.

Cut in half, dip in juices and enjoy!

SERVE WITH

Potato Salad with Bits of Bacon (page 105)

It's-Up-to-You New Yorks

Serves 4

What will it be?

A rare and juicy New York steak topped with caramelized onions soaked in Jet Black Peppercorn Sauce with a hint of vermouth, or the same steak slathered with Giant Mushroom Brandy Sauce? The Big Apple boasts two pro teams, so it makes sense to have two great choices!

It's completely up to you, New York. We provided recipes for both toppings for a great Sunday Night Football duo (or would that be duel)?

But let's not forget the other fabulous New York state team! Be sure and start this amazing meal off with our Buffalo Mozzarella and Tomato Stack on page 106.

Jet Black Peppercorn and Onion Sauce Ingredients

1	tablespoons butter
1	sweet onion, such as a Vidalia, sliced into thin rings
1	teaspoon black peppercorns, freshly ground (use coarse setting on your pepper mill)
1	cup beef broth
1	tablespoon veal demi-glace (demi-glace can be stored in your refrigerator for future use)
1	tablespoon dry vermouth

Giant Mushroom Brandy Sauce Ingredients

1	tablespoon butter
8	ounces button mushrooms, sliced (buy the largest you can find)
1	teaspoon fresh tarragon (if you use dried tarragon, use only a pinch)
1/2	cup half-and-half
1	tablespoon brandy

Steak Ingredients

2	teaspoons freshly ground black pepper
2	teaspoons kosher salt
4	New York steaks

Sauce Preparation

Choose which sauce you prefer to make!

For the black peppercorn sauce, melt the butter in a medium skillet over medium heat.

Add the onion and sauté until golden brown, about 10 minutes.

Add the freshly ground black pepper, beef broth and demi-glace.

Stir until demi-glace is incorporated then add vermouth.

Bring to a boil; reduce heat to a low boil, stirring frequently until sauce has reduced a bit and darkened and thickened, about 2 minutes.

Set aside until steaks are cooked.

For the mushroom sauce, melt the butter in a medium skillet over medium heat.

Add the mushrooms and sauté until nicely browned, about 3 to 4 minutes.

Add the tarragon, half-and-half and brandy.

Bring to boil; reduce heat to a low boil stirring frequently until the cream has reduced a bit, about 2 minutes.

Set sauce aside until steaks are cooked.

(continued on next page)

The mushroom sauce will not be thick, but the mushrooms will have a wonderful sweet and mellow flavor and will continue to soak up the cream as they sit.

STEAK PREPARATION

For the steaks, sprinkle salt and pepper over both sides of the steaks.

Prepare grill to high heat. Grill steaks 4 to 5 minutes per side or to preferred doneness.

Transfer steaks to individual plates. Reheat sauces over low heat.

For the mushroom sauce, with a slotted spoon, lay even amounts of the mushrooms over each steak and then drizzle a tablespoon of the cream over each. So Gorgeous!

For the black peppercorn sauce, place even amounts of the onions over each steak with tongs and then drizzle 2 tablespoons of the sauce over each. So Sexy!

SERVE WITH

Buffalo Mozzarella and Tomato Stack (page 106)
Baked Potato Bar (page 114) or Vagabond Veggies (page 110)

Running Back Ragu

Serves 10

If you have never attempted to make real Italian ragu, fear not. All you need is time (and a good cut-back lane) while you run back and forth from the kitchen to the television and back again. Or better yet, bring one of your TVs into the kitchen and call some family or friends to help so you can take your sweet time while not missing a single play. This everything-in-the-pot sauce will last up to 3 days in the fridge, and any remaining sauce freezes perfectly, making this the best leftover meal you could possibly muster up.

Prep Coach

1 Braciole is basically an Italian beef roll and it is so easy to make! It is actually easier to make than the meatballs. The braciole can be made a day in advance. Put on a platter, wrap in plastic wrap and keep refrigerated until ready to brown. Or, you can make it while the pasta sauce is simmering.

2 Pork chops, braciole and meatballs are cooked right in the pasta sauce in separate stages, giving the sauce wonderful texture, flavor and color. The chops and braciole offer two engaging appetizers to tide you and your guests over until the sauce is ready for the pasta!

3 Buy good-quality canned tomatoes for the sauce. It is perfectly fine to use whole canned tomatoes, but if you do, chop them up well before adding them to the pot. Ragu goes with so many types of pasta. Purchase your favorite whether spaghetti, rigatoni, ziti, linguini, farfalle, penne…

Braciole Ingredients

1 *(1¹/2-pound) whole flank steak*
3 *garlic cloves, chopped*
2 *tablespoons chopped parsley*
¹/2 teaspoon dried oregano
¹/2 teaspoon pepper
¹/2 cup Italian-style bread crumbs
¹/2 cup shredded cheese (Parmesan, Romano or Locatelli)
1 *egg*

Braciole Preparation

Place the flank steak between 2 sheets of plastic wrap, place on a cutting board and pound with a meat mallet until thin.

In a small bowl, mix the garlic, parsley, oregano, pepper, bread crumbs and cheese. Add egg and whisk with a fork until incorporated and moist. Evenly spread mixture over flattened steak.

Starting at a short end, roll the steak up tightly and then tie every 2 inches with kitchen string so it holds together.

Place on a platter, cover with plastic wrap and store in refrigerator until ready to brown.

(continued on next page)

Meatball Ingredients

1 pound ground beef
1 pound ground pork
1 egg
$^1/_2$ cup Italian-style bread crumbs
$^1/_2$ cup grated cheese (Parmesan, Romano or Locatelli)
$^1/_2$ teaspoon thyme
2 tablespoons chopped parsley
1 tablespoon tomato paste
1 small package of pine nuts (4 nuts per meatball)—optional

Meatball Preparation

In a large bowl, mix ground beef, ground pork and egg with a wooden spoon. Add the remaining meatball ingredients, except for the pine nuts, and mix well with your hands.

Using about $^1/_3$ cup of mixture at a time, form round balls and place them on a platter (makes about 10 to 12 meatballs).

(Optional—Take each meatball and using one finger, insert 4 pine nuts into the center of each meatball. Roll each meatball in your hands to reform and seal in the pine nuts.)

Cover with plastic wrap and store in refrigerator until ready to brown.

Braciole and Meatball Browning

This can either be done ahead or while the pasta sauce simmers.

In a large skillet, heat 2 tablespoons olive oil over medium-high heat and brown braciole on all sides, about 2 to 3 minutes per side or 8 to 12 minutes total.

Transfer to a clean platter when done.

In same skillet, brown meatballs (in batches if necessary), on all sides (top, bottom and then 2 sides) about 2 minutes per side or 8 minutes total.

Transfer to a clean platter when done.

If necessary, cover browned braciole and meatballs in foil and place in the refrigerator until ready to add to the sauce.

Pasta Sauce Ingredients

2 tablespoons olive oil
1 large onion, finely diced
3 large carrots, finely diced
3 large celery stalks, finely diced
4 garlic cloves, minced
1 cup red wine
1 (6-ounce) can tomato paste
1 teaspoon each dried oregano, thyme, rosemary and crushed red pepper flakes
1 teaspoon salt
4 (28-ounce) cans crushed or diced tomatoes with juices
3 bone-in pork loin chops
1 or 2 loaves of good crusty Italian bread
Your favorite uncooked pasta— figure 2 ounces per person

Pasta Sauce Preparation

In an 8-quart stockpot, heat olive oil for about 30 seconds over medium heat.

And add onion, carrots and celery and sauté until very soft, approximately 15 to 20 minutes.

Add garlic and sauté 1 minute.

Add wine and tomato paste and stir together for 1 minute.

Add oregano, thyme, rosemary, red pepper flakes and salt and sauté another minute.

Stir in all of the tomatoes, bring to a boil and then reduce heat to a simmer.

Add pork chops.

Cover pot with a tight-fitting lid and simmer for 1 hour, stirring occasionally.

21

(continued on next page)

Remove string from braciole and slice into 1-inch rounds.

Serve a slice of braciole on Italian bread as an appetizer for your guests.

FINALE!

After sauce has cooked for 3 hours or more (at this time both the pork and the braciole have been cooked, removed from the sauce and enjoyed as appetizers), add the browned meatballs.

Increase heat to a low boil. Reduce heat again to simmer, replace the lid and allow meatballs to cook for 35 to 45 minutes or until done.

While meatballs are simmering, cook your favorite pasta according to package directions.

Remove meatballs to a clean serving platter.

Drain pasta and divide among plates or bowls.

Pour desired amount of sauce over the pasta and add a meatball on the side.

ENJOY THE PORK CHOPS!

After letting the sauce simmer for 1 hour, take out pork chops (you may need to search around as some of the meat may have fallen off the bone).

Discard bones. Cut or shred pork into small pieces.

Cover and continue to simmer the pasta sauce while you are enjoying the pork.

Serve the pieces of pork on slices of Italian bread with a spoonful of the sauce as an appetizer for your guests.

AN HOUR LATER— ENJOY THE BRACIOLE!

After you have served the pork appetizer, add the browned braciole with cooking tongs to the sauce and increase heat to a low boil. Reduce heat to keep sauce at a simmer, replace the lid and allow meat to cook for 1 hour, gently stirring occasionally.

After an hour, remove braciole to a cutting board and let rest for 5 minutes.

Cover and continue to simmer the pasta sauce for an additional hour while you are enjoying the braciole.

Very Veggie Beef Stew

Serves 8 to 10

Not getting enough of your daily vegetable requirements? Try this hearty stew, and you will have day's worth of healthy eating. Plus, it gets even better when stored in the refrigerator for leftovers.

Ingredients

2   tablespoons oil
1¹/2 pounds stew meat, cut into
      1-inch cubes
2   large onions, chopped into
      2-inch pieces
2   cups ¹/2-inch celery pieces
2   cups button mushrooms, sliced
¹/2 cup red wine
¹/2 cup flour
6   cups beef broth
1   (14-ounce) can diced tomatoes
3   large carrots
2   large russet or red potatoes
1   cup frozen lima beans
1   cup frozen corn
³/4 cup frozen peas

Preparation

Heat 1 tablespoon oil in a large
   pot over high heat. Add stew
   meat and cook until browned,
   about 6 minutes. Remove
   meat to a bowl and set aside.
   Turn heat down to medium.
Add 1 tablespoon oil to the pot.
   Add the onions, celery and
   mushrooms and sauté for
   8 minutes or until soft and
   lightly browned.
Add wine to deglaze the pot. Cook
   and stir for another minute.
Add beef to the pot. Add the flour
   and stir for 1 minute.
Add the beef broth and tomatoes and
   stir well to blend in the flour.
Bring to a boil. Reduce heat to
   simmer and simmer, covered with
   a tight-fitting lid, for 2 hours.
While stew is simmering, peel carrots
   and chop into 1-inch pieces.
Peel and chop potatoes into 2-inch
   pieces (about 3 cups).
Remove lima beans, corn and peas
   from the freezer to thaw.

After stew has simmered 2 hours, add
   the carrots, potatoes and lima
   beans; bring stew back to a
   simmer. Simmer 30 minutes.
Add the corn and peas and simmer
   for a couple of minutes to heat
   them through.

Serve with

Mozzarella and Roasted Garlic Bread
   (page 95)

TRADITIONAL (OH SO!) OSSO BUCO

Serves 4

Veal shanks are another wonderfully flavorful type of meat that is fabulous when slow cooked. Osso buco is prepared almost exactly like our beef short ribs . . . browned and then braised in liquid until it's melt-in-your-mouth tender. Most osso bucco recipes are simmered on top of the stove rather than in the oven. Osso buco is traditionally served over risotto, so we have included a delicious recipe for Mushroom Risotto on page 107 for your enjoyment!

INGREDIENTS

$1^1/_2$ cups flour
1   teaspoon salt
1   teaspoon pepper
2   tablespoons olive oil
8   veal shanks about 2 inches thick
4   garlic cloves
1   onion, coarsely chopped
3   carrots, peeled and coarsely chopped
2   celery stalks, chopped

1   cup marsala wine
1   (14-ounce) can chicken broth
1   (14-ounce) can diced tomatoes
2   tablespoons chopped fresh parsley
1   tablespoon chopped fresh thyme
2   bay leaves
$^1/_2$ teaspoon salt
$^1/_2$ teaspoon pepper
Gremolata (page 25)

PREPARATION

Add flour to a large bowl and stir in 1 teaspoon each salt and pepper. Dredge shanks in flour on all sides.

Heat the oil in a large stockpot over medium heat for about 1 minute.

Add shanks with tongs in batches to brown on all sides, about 4 to 5 minutes per side. Add more olive oil or spray the pot with some cooking spray if necessary while browning.

Transfer browned veal to a platter.

Add garlic, onion, carrots and celery to the same pot and sauté until soft, about 8 minutes. Add wine and stir to deglaze the pot for 1 minute, scraping up and saving the browned bits in the pot.

Add the chicken broth, canned tomatoes, parsley, thyme, bay leaves and 1/2 teaspoon each salt and pepper. Stir for another minute.

Add the veal shanks along with any juices from the platter. Bring to a boil; reduce heat to simmer, cover with a lid and simmer for 2 hours.

Prepare the gremolata and set aside.

When veal is done, carefully transfer veal with tongs to a platter reserving juices.

Pour cooking liquid through a strainer over a saucepan and discard solids.

Simmer cooking liquid in the saucepan until ready to serve.

Place a mound of risotto on each plate. Top each with 2 veal shanks, spoon some of the juices over them and sprinkle with the gremolata.

GREMOLATA

Osso buco is traditionally served with gremolata, a mixture of parsley, lemon zest and garlic.

To make gremolata, combine 1/2 cup minced fresh parsley, 2 tablespoons lemon zest and 1 tablespoon minced garlic in a small bowl and mix. Sprinkle over the veal just before serving.

SERVE WITH

Old-Fashioned Iceberg Wedge (page 106)
Mushroom Risotto (page 107)

CLEVELAND APPLE AND PORTABELLO-STUFFED PORK ROAST

Serves 8

How do you like them apples? We love 'em in pies, cobblers, and, well, stuffed in a big ol' pork roast! Ohio produces around 100 million pounds of apples every year. That's a lot of apples! So if you're a Clevelander and have an overabundance of this favorite fall fruit, try this excellent pork roast that bakes up in just 1 hour.

This amazing pork roast is stuffed with apples, portabello mushrooms, and Cambozola cheese. Try spreading the Cambozola cheese on slices of apple as an appetizer while making this fun dish.

PREP COACH

1 For this recipe, you will need 1 whole boneless pork loin roast. Ask your grocer for one long piece, not 2 tied together. You also do not want one that is too thick.

2 Cambozola is a wonderful cheese which tastes like a mix of Camembert and Gorgonzola. It is delicious spread on apples, crackers or toasted bread. It should be available in the specialty cheese section of your local grocery. Blue cheese may be substituted with no problem.

STUFFING INGREDIENTS

1   tablespoon butter
1/2 cup finely diced celery
1/2 cup finely diced onion
3/4 cup chopped portabello mushrooms
3/4 cup diced red apple
1/2 teaspoon rosemary
2 to 3 ounces Cambozola cheese or blue cheese
1   cup fine Italian-style bread crumbs
1/4 cup chopped fresh parsley

PORK INGREDIENTS

1   (3- to 4-pound) boneless pork loin roast (make sure you ask your grocer for 1 whole roast, not in 2 pieces tied together).
1   teaspoon salt
1   teaspoon pepper
1/2 teaspoon rosemary

PREPARATION

Preheat oven to 425 degrees.

To make stuffing, melt butter in a medium skillet over medium heat, then add celery, onion and mushrooms and sauté for 5 minutes.

Add apple and rosemary and sauté for another 2 minutes.

Add cheese, stirring constantly until it melts and incorporates, about 1 minute.

Remove skillet from heat and stir in bread crumbs and parsley; set skillet aside.

Slice pork roast lengthwise, but not all the way through. Slice it far enough so you can fold it open like a book.

Fold open and lay stuffing on one side, pressing it down so it holds together well.

Fold nonstuffed side over stuffed side and tie with string at 1-inch intervals.

Generously sprinkle roast on all sides with the salt, pepper and rosemary.

Place roast in a 9×13-inch baking dish, fat side down.

Bake, uncovered, for 15 minutes at 425 degrees. Bake another 45 to 50 minutes at 325 degrees. Remove from oven and allow to cool for about 5 minutes.

Remove string and slice into 1/4-inch slices. Serve 2 slices per plate.

SERVE WITH

Soy-Roasted Potatoes and Carrots (page 115)

CAROLINA PULLED PORK WITH A THAI TWIST

Serves 8 or more

Want an easy way to serve a crowd of hungry football fans? Slow cook a Boston butt pork roast, shred the meat with a couple of forks, and serve it on buns topped with our delicious Thai Slaw. Pulled pork can be slow cooked with many different liquids, including your favorite bottled BBQ sauce, however the Carolinas are known for using vinegar-based sauces, and we love the results!

PREP COACH

1 When shopping for the pork roast, a cut of pork called the pork shoulder or Boston butt will work great.

2 Make the Thai slaw ahead of time as it tastes better as it sits in the refrigerator.

Pulled Pork Ingredients

1   (4-pound) Boston butt pork roast
3/4   cup teriyaki sauce
1/2   cup cider vinegar
1   onion, coarsely chopped
4   garlic cloves, smashed and
     left whole
1   teaspoon pepper
1   teaspoon paprika
1/2   teaspoon celery salt
8   (or more) hamburger buns or
     Kaiser rolls

Pulled Pork Preparation

Preheat oven to 275 degrees.
Place the pork in a large Dutch oven
     or large baking dish fitted with a
     lid (foil can be used if the baking
     dish does not have a lid).
In a medium bowl, mix the teriyaki
     sauce, vinegar, onion, garlic,
     pepper, paprika and celery salt.
     Pour over the pork. Cover with a
     lid or tightly cover with foil.
Bake for 4 hours or until pork is
     tender and easily falls apart.
While pork is baking, make the
     Thai slaw.
After 4 hours, remove the pork from
     the oven, transfer it to a large

cutting surface and let rest for
     20 minutes. Transfer 1 cup of
     the cooking liquid to a small
     saucepan and keep warm over
     low heat.
Remove the string if pork is tied, and
     pull the pork apart into bite-size
     shreds either by hand or by using
     two forks, pulling the pork in
     opposite directions.
Place pork in a large bowl and stir in
     reserved cooking liquid.
Toast the buns under the broiler,
     if desired.
Serve the pork inside the buns and
     top with desired amount of slaw.

Thai Slaw Ingredients

2   tablespoons peanut oil
2   tablespoons sesame oil
1   teaspoon hot chili oil
2   tablespoons soy sauce
3   tablespoons rice vinegar
1   (1-pound) package shredded
     cabbage with carrots
1/2   cup diced green bell pepper
1/2   cup diced red bell pepper
1/2   teaspoon minced and seeded
     jalapeño chile
1/4   cup chopped fresh cilantro
Salt and pepper to taste

Thai Slaw Preparation

In a small bowl, whisk together the
     peanut oil, sesame oil, hot chili
     oil, soy sauce and rice vinegar.
Place the cabbage, bell peppers and
     jalapeño in a large bowl.
Stir in the dressing until cabbage is
     coated. Add the cilantro and
     lightly toss.
Add salt and pepper to taste. Cover
     and place in the refrigerator until
     ready to serve.

Serve With

Carolina-Style Pork and Beans
     (page 111)

Mighty Missouri BBQ Ribs

Serves 8 to 10

Who does them better, St. Louis or Kansas City? We love BBQ ribs of varying styles, cuts, and preparation methods from all across the country! Even though we have held a summer Rib-Fest for many years and my father's steakhouse featured some outstanding ribs on the menu, we do not proclaim to be experts! So take these recipes with a grain of kosher salt, and feel free to change them up with some of your own tried-and-true tricks of the grill. Because everyone knows if you love football, you love to grill. And from the Southwest to Missouri or from Texas to Virginia, you probably have some mighty powerful opinions on the subject as well.

Here, we teach you how to be a real Gridiron Gourmet with easy-to-follow steps to make tender, juicy, fall-off-the-bone . . . bones! From what cuts to buy, to creating the rub, to applying low, slow smoke to layering on the BBQ sauce when grilling.

Prep Coach

1. There are three easy steps to making great ribs: the rub, the slow smoke and layering on the BBQ sauce when grilling. Most everyone has an outdoor grill. If you don't, you can accomplish layering on the BBQ sauce under the oven broiler without much sacrifice in flavor.

2. Slow, low heat is the key to obtaining tender, juicy, fall-off-the-bone ribs. But what if you don't have a smoker? There are lots of options! Go on-line and research how to create a makeshift smoker. You can find numerous ideas on how to use roasting pans, your grill, or other household items to achieve the affect. Or, of course, you can purchase one. A cast-iron oven smoker can be reasonably priced and is so easy. Two tablespoons of small wood chips are placed underneath a tray, the meat goes on top, a tight lid covers it and the meat is then slow cooked in the oven. The first few times you use an oven smoker, the meat may have a slight metallic taste, but with repeated use this goes away.

3. The most common types of rib meat are the pork spare ribs, baby back pork ribs, country-style pork ribs (actually from the pork butt), or, if you prefer beef, beef back ribs. You can purchase them either whole or cut in half with 6 bones each. Danish baby back pork ribs are sometimes used, however they are not as meaty. The Danish ribs imported from Denmark have 13 ribs rather than the usual twelve.

4. When determining how much to purchase, I like to figure 4 bones per person. If a rack of ribs has 12 bones, 2 racks will feed 6 people easily.

5. The "over-under" on temperature is to keep the smoker over 250 degrees and under 300 degrees.

6. The number of pounds changes depending on the type of ribs you purchase, which is why I like to count about 4 bones per person. This recipe is for 8 to 10 people, but you may simply purchase fewer ribs for less people.

Serve with

New Potatoes with Brown Sugar Glaze (page 114)
Blue Cheese-Broiled Tomatoes (page 115)

RIB INGREDIENTS

1   cup packed brown sugar
1   tablespoon each paprika, coarse
    black pepper and garlic powder
1   teaspoon each kosher salt, celery
    salt and dry mustard
1   teaspoon chili powder (your of
    choice of chipotle chili powder,
    ancho chili powder, New
    Mexican chili powder, cayenne or
    other favorite)
3   racks of ribs—about 8 pounds

BBQ SAUCE INGREDIENTS

3   tablespoons butter
1   large yellow onion, finely chopped
1   jalapeño pepper, cut in half
    lengthwise, seeded and minced
2   garlic cloves, minced
1/4 cup red wine
4   cups ketchup
2   tablespoons apple cider vinegar
2   tablespoons lemon juice
1   tablespoon packed brown sugar
5 to 6 shakes of your favorite hot
    sauce, such as Tabasco
1/2 teaspoon chili powder (your
    choice of chipotle chili powder,
    ancho chili powder, New
    Mexican chili powder, cayenne or
    other favorite)
1/2 teaspoon Worcestershire sauce
1/2 teaspoon liquid smoke (optional)

PREPARATION

Add all rub ingredients to a bowl and mix. Sprinkle the rub mixture onto ribs and rub into the meat with your hands.

Cover ribs in plastic wrap, set them on a baking sheet and refrigerate for 2 hours and up to overnight so that the rub marinates the meat (if you do not have time for this, no worries. Skipping the marinating process is not a problem).

To make the BBQ sauce, melt the butter in a medium saucepan over medium-high heat.

Add onion and sauté until soft, about 5 minutes. Add jalapeño and garlic and sauté for another minute.

Add wine and stir for 1 minute.

Add remaining BBQ sauce ingredients and simmer for 20 minutes, stirring occasionally.

Do a taste test and add other spices, as desired.

Prepare smoker and smoke meat according to directions. Cut each rack in half or in thirds if necessary for them to fit into the type of smoker you have chosen.

If you have an oven smoker, smoke at 275 degrees for 3 hours.

When meat is finished smoking, carefully place ribs on a platter. It is okay if the ribs fall apart a bit because they will eventually be cut into 2-bone sections for serving.

Prepare the grill. Whether using charcoal or gas, only heat the grill to medium heat. You want the meat to stay moist, so do not cook on high heat.

Brush a thin layer of BBQ sauce on top of the ribs. Grill ribs bone side down with the lid on for 10 minutes, basting on a thin layer of sauce on top every couple of minutes or so. Turn ribs over and grill another 10 minutes, again basting with the sauce every few minutes. Turn ribs over and add another layer of sauce to the top of the ribs and grill another 5 minutes or so. Transfer ribs back to the platter and allow to cool 5 minutes.

Cut into 2-bone sections and serve!

Redskin Coq au Vin

Serves 6

If you have never made this fantastically simple French dish, stop what you are doing and make it now! It is easy and so very flavorful. Braising all of the ingredients in red wine colors both the chicken and the vegetables with a soft red tint, but also serves to cook the poultry to juicy fall-off-the-bone perfection. Our recipe adds brussels sprouts along with the traditional onions, carrots, and mushrooms in order to add a bit of color. Impress your guests with it at your next football dinner party!

Prep Coach

Dark meat with skin-on and bone-in are the best cuts for slowly braising chicken pieces, so make sure you choose mostly thighs and legs along with a couple of bone-in, skin-on breasts.

Coq au Vin is French for "rooster in red wine," but nowadays we use the inexpensive cuts of chicken!

INGREDIENTS

Assorted bone-in and skin-on
   chicken pieces (1 or 2 pieces per
   person. We use 4 legs, 4 thighs
   and 2 breasts, or 6 legs and
   6 thighs.)
1   *tablespoon salt*
1   *tablespoon pepper*
4   *slices bacon*
12 *small boiling onions, ends cut*
    and papery skin removed
6   *ounces baby-bella mushrooms,*
    sliced
6   *garlic cloves, lightly mashed*
    and peeled
1   *(14-ounce) can chicken broth*
1   *tablespoon chopped fresh thyme*
3   *cups red wine, or use the whole*
    bottle (An inexpensive burgundy
    or pinot noir is best.)
6   *carrots, peeled and cut into*
    2-inch pieces, or 1/2 pound
    baby carrots
18 *whole brussels sprouts, stems*
    removed
1/4 *cup flour*

PREPARATION

Place chicken pieces on a large
   platter and evenly season them
   with the salt and pepper.
In a large stockpot or Dutch oven
   fitted with a lid, cook bacon until
   well browned and transfer with
   tongs to a paper towel.
Remove pot from heat for a minute,
   allowing the bacon drippings
   to cool.
Return pot to medium-high heat and,
   using tongs, brown chicken in
   batches 2 to 3 minutes per side.
   Return chicken to a clean platter.
Add boiling onions, mushrooms and
   garlic and sauté until browned,
   8 to 10 minutes.
Add chicken broth and stir to
   deglaze the pot for 1 minute,
   scraping up and saving the
   browned bits in the pot.
Chop or crumble the bacon and add
   to the pot. Then add the thyme
   and red wine.
Add the chicken pieces, tucking them
   down into the broth.
Bring to a boil, reduce to simmer,
   cover tightly and simmer for
   20 minutes.

After 20 minutes, using a ladle,
   scoop out about 2 ladlefuls of
   the broth into a small bowl; set
   aside and allow to cool completely
   (this will be used to mix with the
   flour as a thickener for the sauce).
Add carrots and brussels sprouts,
   tucking them down into the
   broth. Bring to a boil, reduce heat
   and continue to simmer for
   another 40 minutes.
Turn off heat and transfer chicken
   with tongs to one or two clean
   serving platters, reserving broth
   in the pot. Place the chicken in
   the center of the platter. With a
   slotted spoon, place all of the
   vegetables around the chicken.
Whisk flour into the small bowl of
   reserved broth until incorporated.
   Add flour mixture to the pot of
   broth, whisk well and bring to
   boil. Boil for 1 or 2 minutes until
   thickened into a sauce.
Pour some of the sauce over the
   chicken pieces and then place
   desired amount in a gravy bowl.
Allow guests to help themselves to
   the chicken pieces, vegetables
   and sauce.

Tennessee Whiskey Chicken Quarters

Serves 4

On any given beautiful fall Sunday, my father would plant himself in a folding chair next to the grill, pour a small glass of whiskey on the rocks, light up a cigar, and make these delicious smoky chicken quarters. When my sister and I had our little friends over for this particular meal, he would call it "chicken with wine" so as not to upset the neighborhood! So the big question is, "During what quarter do you want to eat them?"

Ingredients

4   tablespoons butter
1   cup whiskey
1   teaspoon kosher salt
1   teaspoon dried thyme
1/2 teaspoon cayenne pepper
4   chicken hind-quarters (bone-in, skin-on, leg with thigh pieces)

Prep Coach

1 Does it matter what type of whiskey you choose? Not for the purpose of this recipe. There are many types of whiskey such as bourbon whiskey, rye whiskey, Canadian whiskey, and Tennessee whiskey. Bourbon whiskey can be produced in any state, but Kentucky is the only state that produces a significant amount of it. Tennessee whiskey must be produced in Tennessee and goes through a sugar, maple, charcoal filtration process that makes it very smooth.

2 Watch the grill closely. These hind-quarters flair up easily while being basted with all of the butter and whiskey!

3 Use a good basting brush as you will be slathering on the whiskey butter frequently.

Preparation

In a small pot, melt butter and then add the whiskey and stir to combine.

Sprinkle the salt, thyme and cayenne pepper evenly over both sides of the 4 chicken pieces.

Preheat grill to medium—about 350 degrees if your grill has a temperature gauge.

Place chicken on grill, close the lid and cook for 5 minutes. Brush some of the whiskey butter over each piece, close the lid and let cook for another 5 minutes.

Repeat process, continuing to baste every 5 minutes.

After 20 minutes, turn chicken over and continue to baste every 5 minutes for another 20 minutes or until done.

Serve with

Three Wide Set Mac' and Cheese (page 109)

Green Beans with Feta Cheese (page 110)

Grill the chicken over medium heat or at around 350 degrees. It needs to grill slowly in order to obtain the subtle smoky flavor!

Gary's Louisiana Gumbo

Serves 8 to 10

This recipe comes from my brother-in-law. It is so good that we have never tried any other gumbo recipe. When chopping up the ingredients, reflect on how this great state made it through the Katrina disaster and how the amazing football team gave New Orleans a bit of hope through it all, and won a Super Bowl to boot shortly after in 2009.

Prep Coach

1 Add the shrimp and crab meat to the pot right at the end so they do not overcook.

2 If you choose to add crab to the gumbo, we like to buy precooked king crab legs from the grocer. Crack, remove the crab meat and coarsely chop. Keep refrigerated until ready to add to the pot. Three crab legs should yield a little more than the needed 1 cup. Be sure to handle the crab shells with heavy kitchen towels to protect your hands!

3 The traditional way to use gumbo filé is to sprinkle a bit in each bowl while the gumbo is very hot, stir and let it sit for 5 minutes before eating. I like to put it right in the pot but some say that this changes the texture so that it does not freeze well or reheat well. I have not found this to be true, but please decide yourself on how you would like to add your filé to this wonderful recipe. By the way, gumbo filé is made from the leaves of sassafras trees!

INGREDIENTS

3 tablespoon olive oil
2 boneless skinless chicken breasts, cut into $1/2$-inch cubes
2 boneless pork loin chops, cut into $1/2$-inch cubes
2 andouille sausages, cut into $1/4$-inch rounds
1 large onion, diced
1 red bell pepper, diced
1 green bell pepper, diced
3 celery stalks, diced
3 garlic cloves, minced
$1/4$ cup flour
3 (14-ounce) cans stewed tomatoes with juices, chopped (Use kitchen scissors to chop them up right in the can!)
3 (14-ounce) cans chicken broth
2 cups frozen sliced okra
$1/2$ pound uncooked medium shrimp, peeled, deveined and left whole
1 cup fresh cooked crab meat, coarsely chopped (optional)

SEASONINGS

$1/2$ teaspoon crushed red pepper
$1/2$ teaspoon cayenne pepper
1 teaspoon Worcestershire sauce
3 bay leaves
Salt to taste
2 teaspoons gumbo filé (see PREP COACH)

PREPARATION

Heat 1 tablespoon olive oil in a large 8-quart stockpot over medium-high heat.

Add chicken, pork and sausage and stir until lightly browned, about 8 minutes.

Remove meat from pot to a bowl and set aside.

To the same pot, add 2 tablespoons olive oil over medium heat.

Add the onion, peppers and celery. Sauté until soft, approximately 6 minutes.

Add garlic and sauté 1 minute. Add flour and stir for another minute to incorporate.

Add stewed tomatoes, chicken broth and okra and bring to a boil, then reduce to a simmer.

Add all of the seasonings and simmer for another minute.

Add the browned chicken, pork and sausage and stir to combine.

Cover pot with a tight-fitting lid and simmer for 1 hour, stirring occasionally.

Just before serving, remove bay leaves, add shrimp and bring gumbo to a low boil. Simmer gumbo for 5 minutes to cook the shrimp.

Turn off heat and stir in cooked crab. Ladle into bowls and enjoy.

SERVE WITH

Third Down and Dirty Rice (page 108)

Don't let the very long list of ingredients frighten you. Get friends and family involved in the chopping. After that, it's a matter of throwing it all in the pot, sitting back, and letting the gumbo simmer and stew while you sit and watch the Sunday games!

"Scalloped" New England Chowder

Serves 4

Are you patriotic? Can you name the New England states? If not, you will want to look them up after trying this delicious soup. Our version here offers a whole new way of preparing chowder. First we sauté a beautiful mix of leeks and other vegetables. We then purée the vegetables in a blender, similar to a bisque but without all the heavy cream and fat. It becomes a New England chowder-style soup by adding kernels of fresh corn and scallops. Add a bit of cooked lobster meat as an over-the-top New England treat.

Prep Coach

Don't add the scallops to the soup until everything else is ready. You don't want to accidentally overcook the scallops while rushing around doing the final preparations!

Ingredients

2	ears of corn
3	tablespoons butter
3	leeks (use white and pale green parts only), sliced into rings of medium thickness and rinsed well in a colander
2	tablespoons thinly sliced shallots
1	medium onion, chopped
1	small carrot, peeled and sliced into $1/2$-inch pieces
2	celery stalks, sliced into $1/2$-inch pieces
1	medium russet potato, peeled and chopped
3	garlic cloves, chopped
$1/2$	cup dry white wine, such as sauvignon blanc
$2 1/2$	cups (or more) chicken broth or stock
$1/2$	teaspoon Old Bay seasoning
$1/2$	teaspoon salt
12	medium-size scallops
1	cup cooked lobster meat, cut into bite-size chunks (optional)
$1/4$	cup parsley, chopped

Preparation

Take an ear of corn, stand it on end and carefully slice off the kernels (it helps to do this in a wide shallow bowl so the kernels stay contained). Repeat for the other ear of corn. Set aside corn for later use.

In a 3-quart or bigger stockpot, melt the butter over medium heat.

Add leeks, shallots, onion, carrot, celery and potato and sauté until very soft (do not brown), about 10 to 12 minutes. Add garlic and sauté another minute.

Add wine and sauté until most of the wine has been absorbed.

Add chicken stock, bring to a boil and then reduce to simmer.

Simmer, covered, until vegetables are soft, approximately 20 minutes.

Remove from heat, uncover, and allow soup to cool at least 10 minutes.

When soup has cooled, blend soup in batches in a blender, returning soup to another pot for reheating (blended soup should yield about 5 cups).

(continued on next page)

Stir the soup well and add a bit more chicken broth if the soup is too thick for your preference.

Season the soup with Old Bay seasoning and salt.

Over medium heat, bring soup to a simmer.

Add the corn and scallops and gently stir.

Simmer for about 5 to 6 minutes or until scallops are tender. Do not overcook scallops, as they become rubbery and lose their flavor! Remove chowder from heat.

If you are adding lobster, evenly divide room temperature cooked lobster between 4 bowls.

With a slotted spoon, place 3 scallops in each bowl, then ladle desired amount of soup in each bowl.

Garnish with a pinch of parsley over each bowl.

Feel free to play around with this excellent basic soup recipe by omitting the scallops and corn. Add a cup of broccoli florets or cauliflower florets to the boiling stock for a broccoli or cauliflower soup. Or, add 3 to 4 tablespoons mashed roasted garlic for a rich garlic flavor. Or, add 1/4 cup of canned pumpkin to each blender batch for a pumpkin flavored soup.

Raven About Maryland Crab Cakes

Serves 4

PREP COACH

1   You can either purchase fresh lump crab meat already shelled, or you can buy whole king crab legs and remove the crab meat on your own. If you buy the whole legs, 3 crab legs should yield the needed 1½ cups. Be sure to handle the crab shells with heavy kitchen towels to protect your hands!

2   This recipe is intended to go with Scalloped New England Chowder, so it only serves 4. Feel free to double the recipe for more people or to serve as a main course.

3   Crab cakes tend to be quite salty, so we like to use plain panko (Japanese bread crumbs) which have a great deal less salt then regular bread crumbs and also yield a crunchy texture.

INGREDIENTS

½ cup panko (Japanese
    bread crumbs)
1   egg
2   tablespoons mayonnaise
1   teaspoon lemon juice
1   tablespoon Parmesan cheese
½ teaspoon Dijon or honey mustard

1   tablespoon minced fresh parsley,
    or 1 teaspoon dried
¼ teaspoon Old Bay seasoning
1½ cups coarsely chopped lump
    crab meat
2   tablespoons olive oil
Your favorite tartar sauce or other
    preferred condiment

PREPARATION

Whisk the egg in a medium-size bowl. Whisk in the mayonnaise, lemon juice, cheese, mustard, parsley and Old Bay until smooth.

Add the crab and bread crumbs to the bowl and gently mix until incorporated, being careful not to break apart the nice lumps of crab.

With your hands, form 4 even crab cakes (they will each be approximately 3 inches in diameter) and place them on a platter.

Heat the olive oil in a medium-size skillet over medium heat.

Cook the crab cakes about 3 minutes per side or until browned and crispy.

Serve with a dollop of tartar sauce.

FUN & EASY MONDAY NIGHTS

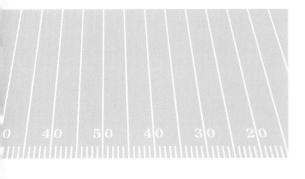

After a hard day at work, you can't wait to get home and watch *Monday Night Football*! The only problem is, you're too tired to cook. Well, here we feature some easy to make football-watching-friendly recipes that will make sure everyone gets fed with no time away from the tube... or flat screen. Go team!

TEXAS TRI-TIP BBQ

Serves 6

Not just Dallas or Houston, but all of Texas is known for their dark and dangerous BBQ sauces, and this is no exception. This sauce has a beautiful dark, almost black, color to it, with a fine kick of heat and a pleasing hint of sweet. After being grilled, the tri-tip is sliced and placed on plates and is divine when served with our colorful succotash vegetable mix either on the side or underneath.

The tri-tip cut of beef has an incredible flavor all its own, cooks up fast, and is super easy to prepare!

INGREDIENTS

1   tablespoon butter
1   small onion, finely chopped
2   garlic cloves, minced
1   cup ketchup
1/2 cup dark molasses
2   tablespoons red wine vinegar
2   tablespoon balsamic vinegar
1/2 teaspoon cayenne pepper
1/2 teaspoon Worcestershire
1   whole tri-tip roast
    (about 2 pounds)

PREPARATION

To make the BBQ sauce, melt the butter in a medium saucepan over medium-high heat.

Add onion and sauté until soft, about 5 minutes.

Add garlic and sauté for another minute.

Add ketchup, molasses, vinegars, cayenne and Worcestershire.

Reduce heat and simmer for 20 minutes, stirring occasionally.

Prepare grill to medium-high heat

Place the tri-tip on a platter and brush both sides with a thin layer of the BBQ sauce.

Place the tri-tip on the grill and grill with the lid off for about 35 to 40 minutes, or to preferred doneness, turning every 5 minutes to brush on another layer of BBQ sauce. The result should be a beautiful dark molasses-colored glaze.

Place tri-tip on a clean platter and allow it to rest for 5 minutes.

Slice the tri-tip across the grain and add to plates as desired.

SERVE WITH

Vagabond Veggies (page 110)

MARK'S MONDAY "DATE NIGHT" VEAL

Serves 2

Cooking for your sweetie while you watch Monday Night Football? *Make this dish and he or she will love you forever. How do I know? Well, it worked for me and has become my favorite "date night" dish (umm . . . other than Mark of course).*

INGREDIENTS

1   teaspoon olive oil
1/2 cup sliced green onions
1   (6-ounce) package button mushrooms, sliced
2   teaspoons minced garlic
1/4 cup red wine
1 (15-ounce) can tomato sauce
1/4 teaspoon oregano
1/4 teaspoon pepper
6   very thin slices of veal (scaloppine)—3 slices per person
1/2 cup milk
1   egg
1   cup seasoned bread crumbs, such as Progresso Italian Style
1   tablespoon olive oil
2 to 4 tablespoons shredded Parmesan or Romano cheese

PREPARATION

To make the sauce, heat 1 teaspoon olive oil in a medium pot over medium-high heat.

Add green onions and mushrooms and sauté until lightly browned and soft, about 8 minutes. Add garlic and sauté one more minute.

Add the wine and stir for another minute.

Add the tomato sauce, oregano and pepper and bring to a boil. Reduce to a simmer, cover and continue to simmer sauce while making the veal, stirring occasionally.

Place the veal between 2 pieces of waxed paper and pound with a meat mallet until thin. Add the milk and egg to a medium bowl and whisk to incorporate the egg.

Add bread crumbs to a dinner plate.

Dredge each veal slice in the egg mixture then the bread crumbs and remove to a platter.

Heat 1 tablespoon olive oil in a large skillet and cook veal, about 3 to 4 minutes per side (in batches if necessary, adding more oil when needed).

Place 3 scaloppine on each plate, spoon desired amount of sauce over and top each with 1 or 2 tablespoons shredded cheese.

SERVE WITH

Asparagus with Grape Tomatoes and Romano Cheese (page 109)

45

BACON, ONION, AND MUSHROOM-STUFFED BURGERS

Serves 6

Any day is the best day of the week for grilling burgers. Don't you love one piled high with bacon, onion, mushrooms, cheese, and, of course, lettuce and tomato? But why put all that stuff on top when you can put it inside? Here is a fun idea for stuffing your hamburgers with all your favorite toppings.

INGREDIENTS

1 teaspoon olive oil
4 ounces mushrooms, chopped
1/2 small onion, finely diced
4 slices bacon, fried until crispy and chopped
Celery salt, garlic powder and pepper

2 pounds ground beef
6 tablespoons grated Cheddar cheese
6 hamburger buns
Ketchup, mustard, slices of tomato, lettuce leaves

PREPARATION

Heat olive oil in a medium skillet over medium-high heat.
Add mushrooms and onion and sauté until soft and browned, about 6 minutes.
Add chopped bacon and sauté for another minute.
Add a couple pinches of celery salt, garlic powder and pepper and stir.
Allow mixture to cool.
While bacon-mushroom mixture is cooling, take the ground beef and evenly divide it into 6 portions. Halve each portion and make twelve 4-inch patties. Using a hamburger ring helps keep the sizes equal.
Spoon 2 to 3 tablespoons of the bacon-mushroom mixture on top of each of 6 patties.
Top each of those 6 patties with 1 tablespoon Cheddar cheese.
Place the other 6 patties on top of the dressed patties and seal edges together well with your hands. Season burgers on both sides with a bit of the celery salt, garlic powder and pepper.

Place burgers on a platter, cover in plastic wrap and refrigerate for about 30 minutes.
Grill patties over medium-high heat until preferred doneness, about 6 minutes per side.
Serve on buns with a tomato slice, lettuce leaf, ketchup, mustard or whatever your preferred condiments may be.

PREP COACH

1 After hamburger patties have been made, cover in plastic wrap and put in the refrigerator until ready to grill. This will help them keep their shape when cooking.

2 The hamburgers will have a tendency to separate when cooking. Don't worry, they still taste great!

SERVE WITH

Italian Antipasto Salad (page 104) or Tri-Color Pasta Salad (page 103)

CHILE CHEESE-STUFFED MEAT LOAF

Serves 4

Did you know that National Meatloaf Day is October 18? Celebrate it this year with our exciting recipe, and you will never find meat loaf boring again! We roll up the ground beef with spicy green chilies and American cheese. It's all easy too, right down to the mushroom gravy and the Creamy Mashed Potatoes on page 113.

MEATLOAF INGREDIENTS

1 1/2 pounds ground beef
1   egg
3   tablespoons ketchup
1/2   cup fine seasoned bread crumbs,
      such as Progresso Italian Style
1/2   teaspoon parsley flakes
1/2   teaspoon salt
1/4   teaspoon pepper
3   slices American cheese
      (each 3 1/2-inch square),
      sliced into 1-inch strips
1   (4-ounce) can diced roasted
      green chilies

MUSHROOM GRAVY INGREDIENTS

3   tablespoons flour
1   (14-ounce) can beef broth
1   tablespoon butter
6   ounces mushrooms, sliced
Salt and pepper

PREPARATION

Preheat oven to 350 degrees

Add ground beef, egg, ketchup, bread crumbs, parsley flakes, salt and pepper to a large bowl and mix well with a wooden spoon.

Cut a large sheet of waxed paper and place it on your work surface.

Take the ground beef mixture with your hands and press it into a rectangle on top of the waxed paper. The rectangle should be approximately 7×11 inches.

Evenly lay the strips of American cheese over the center of the beef in one layer.

Evenly sprinkle the green chilies over the cheese.

Starting with one of the short ends, roll up the meat loaf, pushing up the waxed paper as you roll to help keep the loaf together. You will need to gently push the cheese back into the meat loaf with your fingers as you roll. Discard the waxed paper.

Pinch the ends together and reform with your hands, sealing any open areas.

The loaf should be about 4×8 inches.

Place meat loaf in an 4 1/2 × 8 1/2-inch ungreased loaf pan.

Bake at 350 degrees for 1 hour.

While meat loaf is baking, prepare the gravy.

In a small bowl, whisk the flour and beef broth together. Melt butter in a small saucepan over medium high heat. Add mushrooms and sauté for 5 minutes. Whisk the broth and flour mixture into the mushrooms. Increase heat to high and bring to a boil while whisking constantly until gravy is smooth and thickened. Season to taste with salt and pepper. Keep warm until ready to serve.

Remove meat loaf from oven and allow to cool in the pan for 10 minutes.

Remove meat loaf with a spatula, transfer to a platter and allow to cool for another 5 minutes. Slice into 4 large pieces.

Place meat loaf on 4 individual plates, pour gravy over and serve with mashed potatoes.

SERVE WITH

Creamy Mashed Potatoes (page 113)
Sugar Snap Peas with a Cashew Crunch (page 113)

Substitute the pork and beef broth with chopped uncooked chicken and chicken broth, or peeled uncooked shrimp and vegetable broth!

Quick-Hitter Stir-Fry

Serves 4

The key to a really great quick-hitter run play is to surprise the defense by quick-snapping and going right at them. In the same way, the key to a really great stir-fry is to not be afraid to go right at the stir-fry! No need for a wok or any special equipment. Just keep that skillet at high heat, turn on the hood or air vent to keep the smoke at bay and add the ingredients in stages, stirring them as you go. If you are a stir-fry novice, use a nonstick skillet. A good nonstick skillet is a dream to work with, does an excellent job of cooking the ingredients at high heat, and requires less oil. The other trick to a great stir-fry is the sauce. Not too much, because you do not want to drown the beautiful veggies, and the sauce should have a good mix of sweet, salty, and savory flavors.

Sauce Ingredients

3/4 cup beef broth
2 tablespoons oyster sauce
1 tablespoon rice vinegar
1 tablespoon soy sauce
1 tablespoon honey
1 teaspoon sesame oil
1/4 teaspoon crushed red pepper
1 tablespoon cornstarch

Stir-Fry Ingredients

1 tablespoon vegetable or olive oil
1 cup 1-inch onion pieces
1 cup 1/2-inch carrots pieces
2 large boneless pork loin chops, cut into 1/2-inch bite-size pieces
1 green bell pepper, cut into 1-inch pieces
1 cup (heaping) fresh 1-inch broccoli pieces
1 cup shiitake mushrooms, sliced thin and stems removed
1/2 cup cashews
Salt and pepper (optional)

Preparation

Add all sauce ingredients to a small bowl, whisk until incorporated and set aside.

Heat 1 tablespoon oil in a large skillet over high heat.

Add onion and carrots (they should sizzle in the pan) and stir-fry 3 minutes.

Add pork and bell pepper and stir-fry 2 minutes.

Add broccoli and mushrooms and stir-fry 3 minutes.

Add sauce and cashews and turn off heat.

Stir for another minute to blend flavors and thicken.

Season to taste with salt and pepper, if desired.

Remove from heat and serve over your favorite rice.

Serve With

Sesame Jasmine Rice (page 108)

51

Pinto Pork Enchiladas

Serves 6

Enchiladas are great for Monday Night Football! They're tasty, meaty, cheesy, and most importantly for game night after work—easy.

Six (8-inch) flour tortillas fit perfectly side by side in a 9×13-inch baking dish. The only cooking required is to sauté the pieces of pork and onion. Other than that, it's just a matter of throwing everything into a tortilla and baking them for 20 minutes or so. Game on!

INGREDIENTS

1   tablespoon olive oil
3   boneless pork loin chops, cut
     into 1/2-inch bite-size pieces
1   large white or yellow onion,
     chopped
1   (15-ounce) can pinto beans,
     rinsed and drained (a can of
     3-bean blend of pinto, black
     and kidney also works well)
1   (4-ounce) can diced green
     chilies
1/2 cup sour cream
1/2 teaspoon salt
1/2 teaspoon pepper
6   medium (8-inch) flour tortillas
1   cup purchased enchilada sauce
1   cup shredded Monterey Jack or
     Cheddar cheese or a blend
     of both
1/2 cup fresh tomatoes, diced
     (optional for garnish)

PREPARATION

Preheat oven to 350 degrees.

Heat the olive oil in a medium skillet over medium-high heat.

Add the pork and onion and sauté until nicely browned and cooked through, about 10 minutes. Turn off heat.

Add the beans, green chilies, sour cream, salt and pepper and stir until sour cream is incorporated.

Place a tortilla on a flat work surface and pour 2/3 cup of the pork mixture down the center. Roll the tortilla up and put it in a 9×13-inch baking dish (place it on one of the short sides of the dish as the 8-inch tortilla should fit perfectly)

Repeat with remaining 5 tortillas, adding them to the baking dish in one layer.

Evenly pour the enchilada sauce over the top of the tortillas (they will not be completely covered), then evenly sprinkle the Monterey Jack or Cheddar cheese over the top.

Bake, uncovered, at 350 degrees for 20 to 25 minutes.

Place one enchilada on each of 6 dinner plates and garnish with fresh tomatoes.

SERVE WITH

Gridiron Guacamole (page 98)
Spinach Con Queso Dip

Pigskin-in-the-Pocket Chicken Breasts

Serves 4

Most quarterbacks focus intently on getting the pigskin out of the pocket in 3 to 4 seconds. Here's a way to turn that around by getting the ham into the pocket of this delicious and fun dish.

Stuffing a chicken breast is a fun and easy way to add flair and presentation to your meal. Our Prep Coach gives easy instructions on how to cut the pockets, and after that, stuffing the ingredients inside is a cinch. Feel free to experiment with all kinds of stuffing ingredients. You almost can't go wrong!

Prep Coach

1 To make an opening in the chicken, place the breast on a cutting board and using a sharp knife, cut a 1- to 2-inch opening in the thickest part.

2 Then, take your knife and lay it flat in the opening and slice gently in both directions to create a pocket the full length of the chicken breast, but be careful not to cut through or make any other openings in the meat. The opening should still be about 1 to 2 inches wide when you are done.

3 If you happen to cut through the meat in an area or two, don't worry. The recipe will still look and taste great.

Chicken Ingredients

4   boneless skinless chicken breasts
1   thick-cut slice of ham, about
     1/4 pound (your grocer can cut
     a piece for you to take home)
1   teaspoon plus 1 tablespoon
     olive oil
3/4   cup diced yellow onion
1/2   teaspoon thyme
1/4   teaspoon pepper
1/2   cup fine seasoned bread crumbs,
     such as Progresso Italian style
1   tablespoon soy sauce
1   tablespoon Parmesan cheese

Sauce Ingredients

1   (14-ounce) can chicken broth
3   tablespoons flour
2   tablespoons vermouth or sherry

Chicken Preparation

Cut pockets in each chicken breast as noted in PREP COACH.

Chop the ham into dice-size pieces.

In a small skillet, add 1 teaspoon of the olive oil over medium-high heat.

Add onion and sauté until soft, about 5 minutes.

Add the diced ham, thyme and pepper and sauté for another minute.

Remove skillet from heat and stir in bread crumbs.

Add soy sauce and stir for another minute. Stir in cheese. Allow stuffing to cool.

Then, using your hands, stuff each breast with about 1/3 cup of the stuffing, pushing the stuffing into the opening and spreading inside evenly.

In another large skillet that will fit the 4 chicken breasts and that is fitted with a lid, add the other tablespoon olive oil over medium high heat.

Add chicken and, using tongs, brown each side, 2 minutes per side.

Turn chicken over, cover with a lid and cook one side for 4 to 5 minutes. Turn over again, cover with a lid and cook for an additional 4 to 5 minutes or until cooked through.

When chicken is done, remove pan from heat and transfer chicken to a platter or individual plates, reserving any juices in the skillet.

Sauce Preparation

To make the sauce, whisk the chicken broth and flour together in a bowl.

Add the vermouth or sherry to the skillet with the pan juices and turn heat to medium-high. Stir for 1 minute, scraping up and saving the browned bits in the skillet.

Pour the broth mixture into the skillet and bring to a boil until sauce has thickened, whisking for a minute or two.

Pour desired amount of sauce over chicken.

Serve With

Cheesy Cauliflower (page 112)

Totally Retro Chicken Casserole

Serves 4 to 6

We bet your mom made this chicken and rice casserole for you when you were a kid and that it's still one of your favorite dishes. You might be too embarrassed to admit it, but go on! Make it tonight and it'll surely put a big ol' youthful smile on your face.

Ingredients

2 uncooked boneless skinless chicken breasts, cut into 1/2-inch bite-size pieces

2 cups fresh uncooked 1/2-inch broccoli pieces

1 cup Texmati brown rice, uncooked

1 (10 3/4-ounce) can cream of mushroom soup

1 (10 3/4-ounce) can cream of chicken soup

1 (10 3/4-ounce) can cream of celery soup

2 cups water

Preparation

Preheat oven to 350 degrees

Add all ingredients to a large bowl and stir them together thoroughly.

Spray a 9×13-inch baking dish with cooking spray.

Add all ingredients to the baking dish and cover tightly with foil.

Bake in the oven for 1 1/2 hours. Remove from oven and stir.

Cover with foil again and place the dish back in the oven. Bake for another 30 minutes.

Remove from oven, remove foil cover, stir and allow the dish to sit for 15 minutes (this is important as it allows the dish to set and cool).

Serve with

Sweet Bean Salad (page 104)

This dish takes 2 hours to bake and 15 minutes to cool because the rice is not pre-cooked. Using the uncooked rice gives added flavor and creaminess to the dish.

Fabulously Fast Chicken Fajitas

Serves 6

Nothing looks more spectacular during a football game than seeing a wide receiver with 4.3 speed streaking down the field and making a 50-yard catch behind the cornerback or safety. That's fabulously fast just like our fajitas! In addition, nothing smells better than the sizzling ingredients that go into making fajitas . . . can't you already smell those peppers, onions, mushrooms, and chili powder? Stuff like this is why everyone always ends up in the kitchen.

Ingredients

1   cup sour cream
1   jar of your favorite salsa
1   (8-ounce) package shredded Mexican cheese blend or shredded Cheddar cheese
Medium (8-inch) flour tortillas— count 1 or 2 per person
2   teaspoons olive oil
1   green bell pepper, cut into medium strips
1   red bell pepper, cut into medium strips
1   large onion, sliced into medium rings
1   (6-ounce) package mushrooms, sliced
3   boneless skinless chicken breasts, cut into 1/2-inch bite-size pieces
2   teaspoons chili powder
1/2 teaspoon salt

Preparation

Place sour cream, salsa and cheese in separate serving bowls.

Place 1 or 2 tortillas on 6 separate serving plates.

Heat olive oil in a large skillet over high heat.

Add bell peppers and onion (mixture should sizzle in the pan).

Sauté until lightly charred, about 6 to 8 minutes.

Add mushrooms, chicken, chili powder and salt and sauté, stirring frequently until chicken is cooked through, about 5 minutes.

Remove from heat. Using tongs, add about 1/2 cup of the chicken mixture to each tortilla. Top with a tablespoon or two of sour cream, 2 tablespoons salsa and 1/4 cup shredded cheese.

Roll up or fold each tortilla in half and enjoy.

Serve With

Corn and Bell Pepper Salsa Fresca (page 99)

The fajita ingredients cook up in the pan in only a little over 10 minutes, which makes this a fabulously fast weeknight feast.

57

Cool California Chicken Caesar Salad

Serves 4

The Oakland and San Francisco areas of California just have too much excellent food. The amount of fruits and vegetables grown in the state of California is mind boggling, with a list too long to even attempt to give credit. This absolutely heavenly salad, however, gives us a great start. Sourdough croutons, avocado, white wine, and garlic bring a nice California twist to this delicious Chicken Caesar Salad.

Caesar Dressing Ingredients

- $1/3$ cup olive oil
- 1 tablespoon anchovy paste
- 1 tablespoon mayonnaise
- 1 tablespoon white wine, such as chardonnay
- 1 tablespoon white wine vinegar
- 1 teaspoon lemon juice
- 1 teaspoon honey mustard or Dijon mustard
- 1 garlic clove, minced
- $1/4$ teaspoon pepper
- $1/4$ teaspoon Worcestershire sauce
- $1/4$ teaspoon garlic powder
- $1/2$ teaspoon honey for a bit of sweetness (optional)

Salad Ingredients

- 4 boneless skinless chicken breasts
- 1 tablespoon olive oil
- 6 to 8 cups coarsely chopped romaine lettuce
- 1 cup of your favorite croutons (see page 59)
- $1/4$ cup grated or shredded Parmesan cheese
- 2 avocados, coarsely chopped

Preparation

Add all dressing ingredients to a medium bowl and whisk thoroughly. Refrigerate until ready to use.

Place chicken breasts on a platter.
Pour 2 tablespoons of the Caesar dressing onto the chicken breasts and, using a basting brush, brush the chicken on both sides with the dressing.
Either grill the chicken or cook it stovetop. Here is the recipe for stovetop:

Heat 1 tablespoon of olive oil over medium heat in a large skillet that will fit the 4 chicken breasts and that is fitted with a lid.
Add chicken and, using tongs, brown each side, 2 minutes per side.
Turn chicken over, cover with a lid and cook one side for 3 to 4 minutes. Turn over again, cover with a lid and cook for an additional 3 to 4 minutes or until cooked through.
When chicken is done, transfer to a clean work surface and allow to cool for about 5 minutes.

While chicken is cooling, add lettuce, croutons and Parmesan cheese to a large bowl.
Add remaining dressing (or desired amount) to the lettuce and toss.
Divide salad among four individual serving plates.
Slice each chicken breast in $1/4$-inch slices and lay 1 sliced breast over each plate.
Evenly sprinkle chopped avocado on top of each plate.

Make your own croutons. Cut up 2 or 3 slices of sourdough bread into 1-inch pieces and place them on a cookie sheet. Generously spray them with butter spray. Sprinkle them with a bit of salt, pepper and dill (or other spices as desired) and bake at 350 degrees for 15 minutes or until toasted and crunchy.

FLORIDA FISH TACOS WITH CUBAN SPICES

Serves 6

These delicious fish tacos take a Florida spin with some basic Cuban spices such as oregano, crushed bay leaves, cumin, and garlic. The tilapia fish is very lightly breaded and panfried, then sliced and served in soft taco shells topped with Manchego (a delicious cheese from Spain), avocado, salsa verde (green salsa), and fresh cilantro!

Cook extra tilapia fillets for leftovers and serve them whole on Hoagie buns or inside whole lettuce leaves topped with some of the coleslaw. Yum!

Prep Coach

There is no need to ruin a beautiful piece of fish and no need to layer on fat and calories by dipping the fish in egg, then flour, then egg, then bread crumbs and then frying it in a quart of oil! Here, the fish is merely dipped in milk, lightly coated in bread crumbs once, and panfried in only 2 tablespoons of butter or olive oil.

Ingredients

1   (14-ounce) bag of coleslaw
1   (8-ounce) bottle of coleslaw dressing
3/4 cup milk or buttermilk
4   tilapia or other type of white fish fillets
3/4 cup fine bread crumbs
1/2 teaspoon oregano
1/2 teaspoon crushed bay leaves
1/4 teaspoon cumin
1/4 teaspoon garlic powder
1/4 teaspoon salt
2   tablespoons butter or olive oil or 1 tablespoon of each
Small (6-inch) flour or corn tortillas— will need 12 to serve 6 people

Preparation

Place coleslaw in a large bowl, add the dressing and mix well. Refrigerate until ready to serve.

Place your choice of garnishes in small separate serving bowls and refrigerate.

Place milk in a large bowl and add fish fillets. Let soak for a minute or two.

Mix bread crumbs, oregano, crushed bay leaves, cumin, garlic powder and salt and spread on a dinner plate.

Dredge each fillet in the bread crumbs and place on a platter.

Heat butter in a large skillet over medium heat until melted; swirl pan and add fish. Sauté until cooked through but still moist— about 3 to 4 minutes per side.

Transfer fish back to platter and set out garnishes and coleslaw.

Slice fish into bite-size pieces.

Place 2 tortillas on each of 6 plates. Divide pieces of fish among each tortilla, top with 2 tablespoons coleslaw and garnishes and fold in half.

Enjoy some coleslaw on the side.

Garnishes

Lemon or lime wedges
Fresh tomatoes, chopped
Shredded Manchego cheese
Diced avocado
Fresh chopped cilantro
Purchased salsa verde (green salsa such as Herdez)
Hot sauce

SUPER SIMPLE SEATTLE SALMON

Serves 6

PREPARATION COACH

1 You can of course make this meal with any size salmon. Figure that 1 pound of salmon serves about 4 people, with 4 ounces per person. Adjust how much crème fraîche (pronounced *crem fresh*) you use and slightly adjust the cooking time.

2 You will need about 5 ounces of crème fraîche. So if you can find a smaller container, that is good. Crème fraîche can be found in either the dairy or cheese section of large or gourmet supermarkets. It is delicious and can be used for so many things—it is sort of in-between sour cream and whipped cream.

Seattle and Washington state are well known for their love of salmon. If you have ever bought salmon at Pike Place market in Seattle, you would wonder whether many of the mongers had played football in their youths as they throw the large fish around the market with ease and accuracy. I have never seen one hit the floor! With such versatility and ease of preparation, Americans are eating more and more salmon during their busy work weeks. This is an excellent recipe to serve for a dinner party as it is basically foolproof and cooks up in minutes.

INGREDIENTS

1   (1^1/2-pound) whole piece boneless skinless salmon fillet
^{1}/4 teaspoon salt
^{1}/2 teaspoon pepper
1   (8-ounce) container of crème fraîche
^{1}/4 teaspoon dill
4   garlic cloves, minced
2   tablespoons capers

PREPARATION

Preheat oven to 325 degrees.
Place salmon on a large baking sheet that has edges so juices do not run over.
Sprinkle with salt, pepper and dill.
Using a large flat knife, spread about 5 ounces of the crème fraîche over entire salmon.
Sprinkle garlic and capers over the top
Bake salmon for 20 to 25 minutes or to desired doneness (do not turn). The crème fraîche will melt a bit as the fish cooks.

SERVE WITH

Shrimp and Avocado Salad (page 103)
Broccoli with Almond Browned Butter (page 111)

Our friend Ann introduced us to this very elegant, but ever-so-easy recipe for preparing a whole salmon fillet.

SAN DIEGO SWORDFISH K-BOBS

Serves 4

Fish K-Bobs just remind us of San Diego. Can't you imagine grilling a delicious aromatic skewer over a beach campfire with the sun setting over the ocean in front of you? Well, back to our backyard reality . . . the sturdy, meaty texture of swordfish makes it perfect for grilling, and it is even better when cut into bite-size pieces, marinated, and skewered with an assortment of colorful veggies. The soy, teriyaki, red wine, and lemon juice marinade is San Diego superb.

The ingredients only need to marinade for a couple of hours because both the fish and the vegetables soak up the flavors quickly.

K-Bob Ingredients

4   large metal skewers, or
    8 smaller ones
2   large swordfish fillets, cut into
    2-inch squares (cut each fillet
    into 8 pieces)
8   whole large button mushrooms
8   large broccoli florets, leaving
    a large stem on each for easy
    skewering
8   whole large cherry tomatoes, or
    4 small Roma tomatoes
2   green or red bell peppers, or one
    of each, cut into 2-inch squares
    (will need 16 pieces)
2   cups of your favorite cooked rice
    (We suggest Sesame Jasmine Rice
    on page 108.)

Marinade Ingredients

1/4 cup soy sauce
1/4 cup teriyaki sauce
1/4 cup red wine
1   tablespoon lemon juice
2   tablespoons olive oil
1/2 teaspoon dill
1/2 teaspoon pepper
1/2 teaspoon garlic powder

Preparation

Add the marinade ingredients to
    a very large bowl and stir
    ingredients together.
Add the k-bob ingredients (fish
    through bell pepper) to the bowl
    and lightly toss to coat. Cover
    bowl with a fitted lid or plastic
    wrap and refrigerate for 2 hours,
    stirring occasionally.
After 2 hours, remove the marinade
    from the fridge and get the
    skewers ready.
With clean hands, load up each
    skewer alternately with 4 pieces
    of fish, 2 mushrooms, 2 broccoli
    pieces, 2 cherry tomatoes (or
    1 Roma tomato) and 4 bell
    pepper pieces (use more skewers
    as necessary to fit all ingredients).
Place the skewers on a large platter
    or baking sheet.
Discard marinade.

Prepare the BBQ grill to medium-
    high heat.
While the grill is heating, make the
    rice according to package
    directions and keep warm.
Grill the skewers 6 to 8 minutes per
    side or to preferred doneness.
Try to turn skewers only once. You
    can use heavy-duty oven mitts to
    turn them over, or you can use
    1 or 2 tongs to do the job.
To serve, add 1/2 cup of rice to each
    plate. With oven mitts, hold one
    end of a skewer over a plate and
    with a fork gently push off each
    piece of food to the plate. Repeat
    with each skewer and plate.

Serve With

Sesame Jasmine Rice (page 108)

STEVE DILLON'S LINGUINI WITH VODKA CREAM SAUCE

Serves 6

We are lucky enough to have fun neighbors. We wander back and forth across the street at all times of the day sharing our busy days, funny stories, business dilemmas, things to borrow (our favorite item being a pile of fake dog poop), but most importantly . . . sharing food and fun.

During one of these casual walk-over's, Steve made the most incredible pasta dish ever! We loved this dish so much that we made him make it for us a few weeks later so we could sit and take notes. And now we get to share it with you as one of our favorite Gridiron Gourmet classics. We feature another neighbor's recipe, Maggie's Spinach and Strawberry Salad on page 107, as the perfect salad complement.

PREP COACH

1 Do not substitute onions for the shallots. The shallots offer a sweet, mellow flavor.

2 Steve had a great idea that he put right in his recipe: "You might want to reserve the drained tomato juice in case people want to stand around the kitchen drinking wine for an hour or two to prime their appetites; then you can add it to the sauce if it thickens a bit too much." Sounds like a good idea to us!

INGREDIENTS

4   tablespoon butter
8   ounces button mushrooms, sliced or coarsely chopped (about 2 1/2 cups)
2   whole shallots, finely sliced
4   garlic cloves, minced
2/3 cup vodka
1   teaspoon crushed red pepper
1   cup heavy cream
1   cup canned sliced black olives, drained

1   (28-ounce) can diced tomatoes, drained over a small bowl to reserve juice (reserved juices can equal up to 2 cups)
1   teaspoon salt
1   pound dry linguini
2/3 cup grated Parmesan cheese
2   tablespoon freshly chopped basil for garnish

PREPARATION

In a large pot, melt butter over medium heat. Add mushrooms and sauté 2 minutes. Add shallots and garlic and sauté until soft, about 2 more minutes; do not brown.

Add vodka and red pepper flakes and stir 1 more minute.

Add cream, olives and tomatoes and bring sauce to a simmer.

Continue to heat at a low simmer, uncovered, stirring occasionally for a least 1/2 hour so sauce thickens. Add 1/4 cup reserved tomato juice if sauce becomes too think.

(continued on next page)

Sauté ingredients in a pot large enough to hold the amount of pasta you are making, as the pasta will need to warm with the sauce at the end.

Don't be afraid to cook the sauce longer, but add reserved tomato juice in 1/4 cup increments as needed.

In another large pot, bring 4 quarts of water and salt to a boil. Add pasta and cook to al dente according to package directions.

Drain pasta thoroughly then add it to the pot of vodka cream sauce, keeping the sauce on low heat. Stir to coat for about 1 minute.

Remove from heat, sprinkle in the Parmesan cheese, quickly toss and then transfer pasta to a large serving bowl. Garnish with the freshly chopped basil.

SERVE WITH

Maggie's Spinach and Strawberry Salad (page 107)

67

NAUGHTY AND NICE SHRIMP FETTUCCINI

Serves 4

Low-calorie, zero-cholesterol artichoke hearts get a little naughty when paired with plump shrimp and savory bacon. Add some grated Parmesan cheese and crushed red pepper and well . . . we won't be responsible for the reactions.

INGREDIENTS

20 medium-size shrimp, peeled, deveined and left whole
1 (14-ounce) can artichoke hearts, chopped and reserve the juice in the can
1 cup chicken broth
1/4 cup white wine
2 tablespoons lemon juice
1 tablespoon olive oil
3 garlic cloves, minced
1/2 cup sliced green onions
1 small tomato, diced
1/4 teaspoon salt
2 pinches of crushed red pepper flakes
6 strips bacon, cooked and crumbled or chopped
8 ounces fettuccini
1 or 2 tablespoons butter (optional)
Salt and pepper to taste
1/4 cup seasoned bread crumbs, such as Progresso Italian style
1/4 cup grated Parmesan or asiago cheese

PREPARATION

Preheat oven to 350 degrees.
Evenly lay the shrimp in the bottom of a 9×13-inch baking dish.
Sprinkle the chopped artichoke hearts over the shrimp.
Pour 1/2 cup of the reserved artichoke juice, chicken broth, white wine, lemon juice and olive oil over the shrimp and artichokes.
Sprinkle the garlic, green onions, tomato, salt, crushed red pepper and the crumbled bacon over the top.
Place the baking dish in the oven and bake, uncovered, for 20 minutes.

While shrimp is baking, cook the fettuccini in a large pot according to package directions.
Drain fettuccini in a colander and then transfer it back to the pot.
Remove shrimp from the oven and carefully pour the entire shrimp mixture into the pot.
Place the pot over medium heat and gently stir to warm and coat the fettuccini for 2 to 3 minutes. Stir in 1 to 2 tablespoons butter for added flavor, if desired.
Add salt and pepper to taste.
With tongs, divide the pasta among 4 serving plates and place 5 shrimp on each plate.

With a large spoon or ladle, evenly divide and pour the juices and bacon mixture over each plate of pasta (the sauce is very thin, so be sure to ladle a generous amount).
Sprinkle 1/2 tablespoon bread crumbs and 1/2 tablespoon Parmesan cheese over each plate of shrimp.

MEATY DITALINI

Serves 4

Ditalini is a small tubular pasta that's great for meaty dishes such as this, where the pasta can really tuck itself down into the ingredients. This recipe is similar to a "cheesy mac" type of dish, but rather than mixing a bunch of cheese inside, we just add a bit of Parmesan, Romano, or Locatelli on top. Another easy breezy weeknight dish that is great for eating in front of the TV while watching those Monday night games!

INGREDIENTS

1   cup ditalini pasta (very small tubular pasta)
1   pound ground beef
1   teaspoon olive oil
1   cup diced bell peppers (red, green, yellow or a mix)
1   small onion, diced
1   (6-ounce) package sliced mushrooms
1   (3-ounce) can sliced black olives with juices
1   (14-ounce) can tomato sauce
2   tablespoons ketchup
1/2 teaspoon Worcestershire sauce
1/2 teaspoon pepper
1/2 cup grated Parmesan, Romano or Locatelli cheese

PREPARATION

In a small pot, cook the pasta according to package directions and then drain the pasta in a colander (keep the colander in the sink for the ground beef).

Return pasta to the same pot with the heat off.

In a large skillet, sauté ground beef over high heat until cooked through, about 10 to 12 minutes.

Drain beef in the same colander and let sit there while you cook the veggies.

In the same large skillet over medium high heat, add 1 teaspoon olive oil, bell peppers, onion and mushrooms. Sauté until very soft and browned, about 10 minutes.

Add the black olives, tomato sauce, ketchup, Worcestershire sauce and pepper and stir for 2 minutes.

Add the pasta and ground beef and stir for another 2 minutes.

Serve in bowls or on plates topped with 1 or 2 tablespoons of the cheese.

SERVE WITH

Brussels Sprouts with Shallot Cream (page 112)

The Blackstone Hotel Original Reuben

Your Gridiron Gourmet Sandwiches

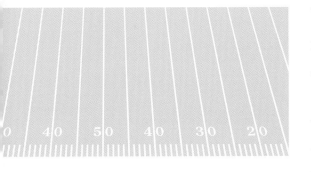

What better time to make to a monster sandwich than right before your team is about to kick-off so you can madly munch away and cheer between mouthfuls? My father owned one of the best steak houses in Omaha, Nebraska. When the restaurant was closed and Dad was doing bookwork, I would have the golden opportunity to raid the walk-in refrigerator and make huge sandwiches piled up with everything but the stainless-steal double kitchen sink.

And speaking of Omaha, Nebraska, did you know that the Rueben Sandwich was invented there? So read on, or rather chop and cook on, to our fabulous sandwich section!

THE BLACKSTONE HOTEL ORIGINAL REUBEN

Serves 4

I bet you never knew that the Reuben Sandwich we all know and love today was named after Reuben Kulakofsky back in the 1920s. Reuben and his buddies would play poker at the old Blackstone Hotel in Omaha, Nebraska, and in order to keep their energy going late into the night, they would create their own sandwiches from the hotel kitchen. We were able to obtain the original recipe from the Junior League of Omaha through their Toast to Omaha *cookbook. This recipe comes from a 1976* Omaha World-Herald *article from the late Bernard Schimmel, son of Blackstone Hotel owner Charles Schimmel. By the way, you can order a copy of the aforementioned cookbook at www.juniorleagueomaha.org.*

THOUSAND ISLAND DRESSING

1   cup real mayonnaise
3   teaspoons chili sauce
1   teaspoon chopped pimentos
1   teaspoon chopped young onion
    (we used green onion)
2   tablespoons minced green bell
    pepper
1/2 cup sour cream
2   hard-boiled eggs (optional)

DRESSING PREPARATION

Blend all ingredients in a blender except the hard-boiled egg. Chop and fold the eggs into the dressing at time of service, if desired.

SANDWICH INGREDIENTS

1   cup sauerkraut, chilled and well
    drained
1/2 cup Thousand Island dressing
8   slices dark rye bread
8   thin slices Emmentaler cheese
1   pound thin slices kosher-style
    cooked corned beef brisket
Room temperature butter

SANDWICH PREPARATION

In a medium bowl, mix the sauerkraut with Thousand Island dressing. Lay 4 pieces of bread side by side.
Place 1 slice of the Swiss cheese on each of the 4 bread slices. Layer with 1/4 pound of the corned beef, then even amounts of the sauerkraut mixture, then 1 more slice of the Swiss cheese. Top with the remaining 4 slices of bread.
Generously spread the top of each sandwich with butter.
Heat a medium-size skillet over medium heat and add one sandwich, butter side down.
Spread more butter on the top side of the sandwich. Press together with spatula and cook (both sides) until browned and hot through so cheese oozes.
Cook remaining sandwiches and eat immediately.

Philly Rib-Eye Cheese Steaks

Serves 4

These delicious sandwiches cook up in no time and are true football fare. Use a good-quality steak such as a rib-eye to make the sandwich melt-in-your-mouth tender. The original cheese of choice for a true Philly cheese steak is, believe it or not, Cheez Whiz! We leave the choice of cheese to you, but we like a bit of Philadelphia cream cheese and white American cheese.

Ingredients

2   rib-eye steaks or other good-quality steaks
2   tablespoons olive oil
2   medium onions, sliced to about 1/4-inch thickness
1   green pepper, sliced thin
6   ounces fresh mushrooms, sliced
1/4   teaspoon salt
1/4   teaspoon pepper
1   teaspoon Worcestershire sauce

4   Italian sandwich rolls or hoagie buns
1   small tub of spreadable Philadelphia cream cheese (optional)
8   slices cheese of your choice— we prefer white American (Cheez Whiz is the true topping, however provolone, American, white American or mozzarella cheese are also used)

Preparation

Slice the rib-eye steaks across the grain into very thin slices (slice as thinly as you can).

Heat 1 tablespoon olive oil in a medium skillet over medium-high heat.

Add the onions and pepper and sauté until soft, about 6 minutes.

Add the mushrooms and sauté another 3 minutes; set aside when done.

In another large skillet, heat the other tablespoon olive oil over high heat.

Add the sliced steak, salt, pepper, Worcestershire sauce and cook, tossing with tongs until desired doneness, about 2 to 3 minutes.

Lay the buns open on a baking sheet.

Spread the top side of each bun with a couple teaspoons of the cream cheese (optional).

With tongs, place desired amount of steak mixture on the bottom side of each bun and then top with the desired amount of pepper and onion mixture. Top each with 2 slices of cheese.

Place cheese steaks under the broiler for a minute or two to melt the cheese and to toast the buns.

Marla's Meatball Subs

Serves 6

Our friend Marla makes the best meatballs around! They are amazingly tender, but manage to hold together well under the pressure of a great big hoagie bun even as it gets tossed from hand to mouth. She says the key is that the ingredients should feel dry while you are forming the meatballs with your hands. What ever you say, Marla, you 'da queen!

MEATBALL INGREDIENTS

1   pound ground pork
1   pound ground beef (extra lean)
2   eggs
1   cup bread crumbs
1   cup grated Romano cheese
1   tablespoon dried basil
1   tablespoon dried oregano
1/2 teaspoon salt
1/2 teaspoon pepper
3   tablespoons water
4   garlic cloves, minced

SAUCE INGREDIENTS

1   tablespoon olive oil
1/4 cup onion, diced
4   garlic cloves, minced
3   (141/2-ounce) cans diced or
    crushed tomatoes with juices
1   (15-ounce) can tomato sauce
1   (6-ounce) can tomato paste
1   cup water
1   teaspoon dried basil
1   teaspoon dried oregano
1/2 teaspoon crushed red pepper
1/2 teaspoon salt

SUB INGREDIENTS

6   hoagie buns
Shredded Romano cheese
    for sprinkling

MEATBALL PREPARATION

In a large bowl, mix ground pork, ground beef and eggs together well with a wooden spoon. Add the remaining meatball ingredients and mix well with your hands.

Form the mixture into 2-inch meatballs—you should yield about 20 meatballs.

Spray a bit of cooking spray in a large skillet. Over medium-high heat, and in batches, brown meatballs 2 minutes per side (top, bottom and then 2 sides) for about 8 minutes total. Allow to cool and then store in refrigerator until ready to add to the sauce.

SAUCE PREPARATION

For the sauce, in a large pot, heat the olive oil over medium-high heat.

Add the onion and garlic and sauté until soft, about 6 minutes.

Add the diced tomatoes, tomato sauce and tomato paste and stir to incorporate. Add the remaining sauce ingredients; stir and bring to a boil.

Reduce to simmer, cover and cook for 2 hours, stirring occasionally.

After 2 hours, add the meatballs to the sauce; bring to a boil.

Reduce to simmer, cover and cook meatballs for 1 hour.

SUB PREPARATION

To serve, slice open the hoagie buns. Place 3 meatballs inside each bun and pour 1/4 cup of the sauce inside each bun. Sprinkle with a bit of Romano cheese.

This recipe serves 6 with a couple meatballs left over. The leftover sauce can be used the next day for pasta!

75

WISCONSIN BEER BRATS

Serves 6

Similar to Detroit and Chicago, Green Bay takes their dogs very seriously. Some top their brats, or in this case their Beer Bratwurst sausages, with sauerkraut, while others say that is a sin. Some boil the brats in the beer, while others say steaming is best. But most everyone agrees that hard rolls or hoagie buns (not typical hot dog buns) and a rich brown mustard (not yellow mustard) are a must. Here we take an Italian slant and top them with sautéed onion, bell pepper, and mushrooms.

INGREDIENTS

2   (12-ounce) bottles or cans of your favorite beer (dark beer is best)
6   bratwurst sausages
1   tablespoon olive oil
1   large onion, sliced into thin rings
1   red bell pepper, sliced into thin strips
1   green bell pepper, sliced into thin strips
8   ounces mushrooms, sliced
6   hoagie buns (do not use hot dog buns)
Good brown mustard (not yellow)
Ketchup

PREPARATION

Pour beer into a medium pot or skillet. Heat beer until steaming but not boiling.

Add brats, cover and cook them for about 15 minutes, keeping them over medium-low heat.

Remove brats with tongs to a platter.

Heat oil in a medium skillet over medium-high heat and add onion, peppers and mushrooms and sauté until very soft, about 15 minutes.

Prepare your grill and set to medium-high heat. Grill brats for about 15 to 20 minutes, turning frequently until well browned and a bit charred in spots. Be sure to keep cooking them until the juices emit and sizzle because that is what will brown them!

Some folks prick the sausages in a couple of places with a fork to get the juices to emit.

If you do not have a grill (or it's too cold outside!), you can cook them in a large skillet, but be sure to turn them frequently and (again) be patient until the juices emit as that is what will get them nice and brown and crispy.

Serve in hoagie buns with brown mustard, ketchup, and onion-pepper mixture on top.

Chicago-Style Hot Dog

Serves 4

Who knew a hot dog could be so complicated? A true Chicago-style hot dog is easy to make, but some of the traditional and unique ingredients are not widely available: a poppy seed bun, a practically florescent bright green pickle relish, and "sport peppers." A sport pepper is a mildly hot green chili pepper that is thin, about $1^1/_2$ inches long and commonly pickled specifically for use on Chicago-style hot dogs. The mix of the hot peppers and sweet relish is divine!

We substitute the poppy seed bun with a sesame seed bun; the bright green relish with regular pickle relish; and the sport pepper with pepperoncini. The buns, relish and sport pepper can be ordered over the internet if you are a purist! Chicago-style hot dogs are also served with small wedges of tomato, chopped onion, and yellow mustard. Brown mustard and ketchup are frowned upon!

Ingredients

4   all-beef jumbo-size hot dogs
4   poppy seed or sesame seed hot dog buns
1   tomato, sliced into 12 wedges
4   pepperoncini peppers, sliced thin (use sport peppers if you can find them!)
A jar of sweet pickle relish
1   large onion, diced
Yellow mustard

Preparation

Boil, panfry or grill the hot dogs according to package directions for the type you have purchased.
Slice open the buns. Add the tomato wedges, hot dogs, pepperoncini, relish, onion and mustard.

MOTOR CITY CONEYS

Serves 6

Coney Island, New York, was the birthplace of the hot dog as we know it today, however, Michigan was the first to create the chili- and onion-covered dog that we today call the Coney Island Hot Dog! The Detroit-style chili is very similar to the Cincinnati Chili recipe we provided earlier in this book, and Michigan folks actually call it a chili dog sauce. If you purchase a good-quality dog and mix up the ingredients at home, controlling the level of salt and fat, these delicious dogs are not too bad for you, either!

INGREDIENTS

6   hot dogs (they should be all beef; the long skinny red type is best!)
6   hot dog buns (try to find a sturdy type to hold the heavy toppings)
1   pound ground beef
1   medium onion, minced
2   garlic cloves, minced
2   teaspoons regular chili powder
1   teaspoon Worcestershire sauce
1/2 teaspoon cumin
1/2 teaspoon paprika
1/2 teaspoon salt
1/2 teaspoon black pepper
1/4 teaspoon cinnamon
1   (6-ounce) can tomato paste
1   cup water
1   tablespoon yellow mustard
Onion, chopped as garnish

PREPARATION

In a large skillet over medium-high heat, cook the ground beef into fine crumbles, using a potato masher if necessary, for about 8 minutes.

Add onion and garlic and sauté another 2 minutes.

Add the chili powder, Worcestershire sauce, cumin, paprika, salt, pepper and cinnamon.

Stir and sauté another minute or so.

Add tomato paste and water and stir well until combined.

Turn heat to low, cover and allow to simmer for 20 minutes.

Stir in the mustard.

Boil, panfry or grill the hot dogs according to package directions for the type you have purchased.

Many recipes say that the hot dog buns should be steamed. You can warm buns in the microwave for 10 seconds, if desired.

Serve hot dogs with desired amount of chili sauce over the dog and then top with a bit of chopped onion as garnish.

This chili sauce recipe yields enough for approximately 6 (1/2-cup) servings.

Recipe can be doubled for more.

HASH MARK ITALIAN HOAGIES

Serves 8 to 10

This is "the" quintessential Italian hoagie and just cannot be beat for ease and expense when feeding a crowd. As much as we respect the numerous chains that make great subs, take time to make your own the next time you have the gang over for football. They will be wowed and wooed and waiting at your door next season. Hint: they can be served on either hash mark!

DRESSING INGREDIENTS

1/3 cup mayonnaise
1/2 cup spicy brown mustard

2 teaspoons olive oil
1 teaspoon white wine vinegar

HOAGIE INGREDIENTS

1 large whole loaf of good Italian or French bread (try to find one that is not too thick)
1 (4-ounce) can sliced mushrooms
1 (3-ounce) can sliced black olives
1 1/2 cups shredded iceberg lettuce
3/4 pound thinly sliced ham
15 thin slices of salami (about 3 ounces)

6 large slices of provolone cheese (about 4 ounces)
2 medium-size tomatoes, cut into 3 slices each (6 slices total)
1 (8-ounce) jar roasted red pepper, cut into long thin slices (you will need 12 strips)

Salt, pepper, oregano

PREPARATION

Whisk all of the dressing ingredients together in a small bowl.

Using a long serrated knife, slice the loaf of bread in half lengthwise.

Working on the bottom half of the bread, sprinkle the mushrooms and olives evenly over the bread (we like to add these on first so they don't topple off).

Evenly lay the shredded lettuce over the mushroom and olives.

Evenly layer the ham over the lettuce. Fold each slice of ham accordion-style so it puffs up a bit.

Evenly layer the salami over the ham.

Evenly layer the provolone over the salami.

Evenly layer the tomatoes over the salami.

Evenly layer the strips of roasted red pepper over the tomatoes.

Add a couple of pinches of salt, pepper and dried oregano on top.

Generously spread the dressing on the top half of the bread; place it on top and firmly press the hoagie together.

Slice into 8 to 10 sandwiches.

INDIANAPOLIS PORK TENDERLOIN SLIDERS

Serves 6

Indianapolis is famous for their great passing offense, a really loud crowd, and breaded pork tenderloin sandwiches, where hunks of pork tenderloin are pounded to thin rounds, breaded, fried, and made into sandwiches. We take a lighter and much easier variation here, where we roast a whole pork tenderloin (the easiest meat in the world to cook), slice it, place it on small buns, top it with onions, cabbage, and Swiss cheese, and then give it a broil in the oven.

ROASTED PORK INGREDIENTS

1   whole pork tenderloin
     (1 to 1 1/2 pounds)
1   teaspoon olive oil
1   teaspoon rosemary
1/2 teaspoon garlic powder
1/2 teaspoon sage
1/2 teaspoon paprika

TOPPING INGREDIENTS

2   teaspoons olive oil
8   thin slices of sweet or yellow onion, each ring cut in half
2   cups shredded tri-color coleslaw
1/4 teaspoon salt
1/4 teaspoon pepper
1   teaspoon brown sugar
6   slices provolone or Swiss cheese, halved to make 12 small slices
12   mini buns or small dinner rolls
Mayonnaise and mustard

PREPARATION

Preheat oven to 350 degrees

Place pork in a long shallow baking dish and drizzle the olive oil over the top.

Sprinkle the rosemary, garlic powder, sage and paprika over the pork.

Roast, uncovered, for approximately 40 to 45 minutes or until a meat thermometer shows 165 degrees.

While the pork tenderloin is roasting, make the topping.

Heat the olive oil in a medium skillet over medium heat.

Add onion and sauté until very soft and golden, about 8 minutes.

Add 2 cups of the coleslaw and sauté until wilted and a bit cooked through, about 2 to 3 minutes. Remove from heat and add salt, pepper and brown sugar and stir.

Place all 12 mini-buns open-face on a large cookie sheet.

When pork is done, remove from oven and allow to rest 5 minutes.

Slice pork into 1/4-inch slices.

Place 1 slice of pork on the bottom half each mini-bun, then top each slice of pork with a generous tablespoon of the cooked slaw; top slaw with a slice of cheese.

Spread desired amount of mayonnaise and mustard on the top half of each bun.

Place under the broiler for a minute or two to melt the cheese and toast the top of the bun.

Assemble sandwiches and place 2 on each of 6 plates.

PITTSBURGH PIEROGIS

Serves 6 (2 per person)

One of the contributors to this cookbook is Canadian and besides taking an occasional glimpse at the CFL, he loves his pierogis! The concept of wrapping dough around a cheese, potato, sauerkraut, or meat filling most likely came from Poland. These little dumplings are traditionally boiled then lightly panfried.

The dough can either be a very plain flour, egg, oil, and water mixture, or can include a bit of sour cream or mashed potatoes.

We include sour cream in our dough as that is the way they love it in Pittsburgh! Our filling offers finely diced panfried potatoes to give the pierogi a bit of texture, and then we add bacon bits and Cheddar cheese for a savory zing. Maybe this is why the state of Pennsylvania produces so many NFL quarterbacks?

Dough Ingredients

2 cups flour
$^1/_2$ teaspoon salt
1 egg
$^1/_2$ cup sour cream
4 tablespoons room temperature
   butter

Dough Preparation

To make the dough, place flour and
salt in a medium bowl. Whisk the
egg in a small bowl; add it to the
flour and stir it in with a fork for
about 1 minute.

Add the sour cream and butter and
cut it in with the fork for another
2 minutes.

Then with your hands, knead the
dough, working in the butter
until you can gather all the
dough and mold it into a ball
that does not separate. This will
take quite a few minutes. Once
you have formed the dough into
a ball, wrap it in plastic wrap and
place it in the refrigerator for at
least 45 minutes.

While dough is chilling, make
the filling.

Filling Ingredients

2 tablespoons butter
$1^1/_2$ cups russet potatoes,
   peeled and finely diced
$^1/_2$ teaspoon salt

$^1/_2$ teaspoon pepper
$^1/_2$ teaspoon thyme
1 tablespoon bacon bits
$^1/_2$ cup grated Cheddar cheese

Filling and Pierogi Preparation

Add 1 tablespoon butter to a small
skillet over medium heat and add
the potatoes, salt, pepper and
thyme. Cook the potatoes until
soft and browned, about 10 to
12 minutes.

Stir in the bacon bits, remove from
heat and allow filling to cool

To finish making the dough, sprinkle
a handful of flour on a small area
of your countertop and rub some
flour on a rolling pin.

Place the chilled dough on the floured
area and roll out dough until it is
a rectangle of about 12 inches by
15 inches. (The rectangle does
not need to be even!)

With a 3-inch biscuit cutter (or a tall
glass works just as well), stamp
12 to 14 circles. Remove the
circles off to the side, and discard
the leftover dough.

Take the filling and place about
1 teaspoon in the center of each
dough circle.

Sprinkle a pinch of the Cheddar
cheese over the filling on
each pierogi.

Fold the dough over the filling to
create a half moon shape. Pinch
each pierogi with your fingers or
with fork tines to seal them
closed. Take care to ensure they
are completely sealed.

Fill a medium pot halfway with
water and bring to a boil. Add
the pierogis and cook for about
2 minutes. You know they are
done when they float to the top!

With a slotted spoon, remove
pierogis to a platter.

Melt 1 tablespoon butter in a medium
skillet and brown pierogis until
light brown, about 2 minutes
per side.

Serve pierogis on a platter with sour
cream on the side.

Bloody Viking BLTs

Serves 4

These towering and ultimately amazing BLTs are topped with slices of hard-boiled egg, red onion, and green pepper . . . and since they cook up quick, they are perfect for a lazy Sunday afternoon brunch. They are even better when served with the perfect wash-down: our Late Morning Hail Marys on page 123!

Prep Coach

1 To boil the eggs, figure 1 egg per person. Place eggs in a medium pot, cover with cool water, add a teaspoon of salt and place the pot over high heat. When eggs come to a boil, reduce heat to simmer and cook for 5 minutes. Allow to cool and then peel. Keep in refrigerator for up to 4 hours until ready to use.

2 It is important to choose the right bread for the type of sandwich ingredients you are using. This sandwich is best with regular wheat, sourdough or pumpernickel bread cut to medium thickness. Take some extra time and buy good bread from a local bakery and have them cut it for you.

Ingredients

16 slices thick-cut bacon
4 hard-boiled eggs
1 head lettuce (iceberg, butter leaf or red leaf)
8 slices wheat, sourdough or pumpernickel bread
Mayonnaise
1 large tomato, cut into 4 slices of medium thickness
1 green bell pepper, sliced into 4 thin rings
1 red onion, sliced into 4 thin rings (reserve remainder for another use)

Preparation

In a large skillet, fry bacon over medium heat until crispy. Transfer with tongs to paper towels, pat off grease and allow to cool (can be made 2 hours ahead).

Boil eggs according to PREP COACH. Slice each egg into 4 rings.

Wash lettuce and tear off 4 large leaves of equal size.

Toast bread in toaster. Spread desired amount of mayonnaise on 4 slices of the toast.

On each of the other 4 pieces of toast, add 4 slices of bacon, 1 lettuce leaf, 1 tomato ring, 4 egg slices, 1 green pepper ring and 1 red onion ring.

Top each sandwich with the mayonnaise toast. Cut each sandwich in half.

Serve immediately.

My Danish mother used to make these sandwiches often on weekends, and so we would like to dedicate this sandwich to the Danish-born field goal kicker Morton Andersen, who currently holds the record for most field goals in NFL history and who played to the ripe old age of forty-eight (also a record). Must have been the Danish Akvavit (also spelled Aquavit), or in this case, the Bloody Marys.

GEORGIA PECAN AND VIDALIA ONION CHICKEN SALAD

Serves 4

Georgia is not only known for their peaches! They produce much of our country's pecans and Vidalia onions as well. This delicious chicken salad showcases the pecans and onions, but also apples, grapes, and almonds. It is so healthy, you might need to pinch yourself to make sure you're not dreaming that it tastes so good. Cutting up the chicken into small pieces helps to keep it deliciously tender while cooking.

CHICKEN SALAD INGREDIENTS

2   teaspoons olive oil
2   boneless skinless uncooked
     chicken breasts, diced into small
     1/4-inch pieces
Salt and pepper
3/4 cup diced apple
1/2 cup thinly sliced seedless
     red grapes
1/4 cup diced celery
1/4 cup diced Vidalia (sweet) onion
1/3 cup finely chopped pecans
1/3 cup sliced almonds

CHICKEN SALAD PREPARATION

In a small skillet, heat olive oil over medium-high heat and add chicken pieces.

Sprinkle in a couple pinches of salt and pepper and sauté the chicken, stirring frequently until cooked through but still tender, about 4 to 5 minutes. Drain chicken in a colander and allow to cool completely.

Place chicken in a medium bowl and add apple, grapes, celery, onion, pecans and almonds.

Add dressing and gently stir to combine.

Serve in rolls or on top of mixed greens.

DRESSING INGREDIENTS

1/3 cup mayonnaise
1   teaspoon walnut oil
1   teaspoon red wine vinegar
1   teaspoon lemon juice
1/4 teaspoon each salt, pepper
     and thyme

DRESSING PREPARATION

Mix dressing ingredients together in a small bowl and refrigerate until ready to use.

Turkey Panini with Gruyère and Tomato

Serves 4

What happens when the defensive end and a linebacker meet at the quarterback? You get the idea: Football Panini! Panini have become super popular and are not very much like the original sandwich that they are named for, but hey, we love what they have evolved into! You do not need a fancy panini press or a grill top addition to your stove to make them either, because they taste just as delicious cooked in a regular fry pan or skillet.

The most common choice of bread is ciabatta, but we prefer slices of good sourdough. Whatever type of bread you choose, make sure it is hearty enough to not become soggy under the tomato slices and grilling process. We think the nutty taste of Gruyère cheese goes great with the turkey.

Ingredients

8 slices sourdough or ciabatta bread
Mayonnaise
Dijon mustard
8 slices Gruyère cheese (purchase a hunk and slice enough to equal 8 regular-size slices)
1 pound roasted turkey breast, sliced thin
2 tomatoes, sliced into 8 rings of medium thickness
1/4 cup room temperature butter

Preparation

Lay all 8 slices of bread on a work surface.

Spread approximately 2 teaspoons (or desired amount) of mayonnaise on 4 of the bread slices and then spread 2 teaspoons Dijon mustard on the other 4 slices.

Place 1 slice of Gruyère on top of each Dijon slice; layer each with 1/4 pound of turkey, 2 slices of tomato and then 1 cheese slice.

Top each with the remaining 4 slices of bread (mayonnaise side down).

Generously spread the top of each sandwich with butter.

Heat a medium-size skillet or grill pan over medium heat and add one sandwich, butter side down.

Press together with a spatula and cook for about 2 minutes. Spread more butter on the top side of the sandwich and flip. Cook another 2 minutes or until well browned and the cheese oozes.

Cook remaining sandwiches and eat immediately.

PREGAME RITUALS

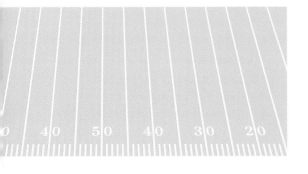

What do your pregame rituals include? A favorite team T-shirt or a kiss on a lucky charm? Doing 100 push-ups or placing a quick call to Mom and Dad? Maybe a rousing game of football in the front yard? If it includes running to the store to pick up your favorite snacks (and we know it does), have a look through our appetizers and be sure to include some of these super tasty ingredients to your list!

SHRIMP PIZZADILLAS (ITALIAN QUESADILLAS!)

Makes 16 to 32 pieces

INGREDIENTS

2   teaspoons olive oil
12 medium-size shrimp, uncooked,
    peeled and deveined
1   red and 1 green bell pepper,
    cut into thin strips
2   large (10-inch) flour tortillas
2   tablespoons sour cream
1   cup shredded mozzarella cheese
2   green onions, sliced thin
1   fresh tomato, finely chopped
Oregano, salt and pepper
Your favorite salsa

PREPARATION

Heat 1 teaspoon olive oil in a large nonstick skillet over medium high heat and sauté all shrimp until cooked through, about 5 minutes.

Remove shrimp to a bowl and set aside.

Add 1 teaspoon olive oil and the red and green pepper to the same skillet and sauté until soft, about 8 minutes.

Remove peppers to a bowl and set aside.

Lay the tortillas out separately and spread 1 tablespoon sour cream over each tortilla.

On *one side* (one half) of each tortilla, layer the following (don't bring ingredients quite to the edge): 1/4 cup of mozzarella cheese, 6 shrimp, 1/2 the red and green peppers, and 1/2 each of the green onions and chopped tomatoes.

Then, sprinkle the remaining cheese over each tortilla (1/4 cup or more).

Starting and ending with the cheese helps hold the quesadilla (or pizzadilla!) together.

Sprinkle a pinch of oregano, salt and pepper over each tortilla.

Fold undressed side of each tortilla over the dressed side and press down a bit.

Add a generous amount of cooking spray to the same large skillet over medium heat.

Add one quesadilla and cook about 2 minutes per side or until heated through and cheese melts (it may help to use two spatulas to assist in turning the quesadillas over in the pan).

Transfer quesadilla to a work surface; cut into wedges and then transfer wedges to a serving tray.

Cook remaining quesadilla, adding additional cooking spray to the skillet as needed.

Serve with a bit of salsa on the side.

Cut each quesadilla into 8 or 16 pieces.

EASIEST PIZZA EVER

Serves variable amount

PREP COACH

1 The pizza "crust" for these super-easy pizzas are matzo crackers, either the salted or unsalted type, whole. Each cracker is about a 7×7-inch square. Find them in the kosher aisle of your grocery store. You will need one whole cracker per person.

2 You can make these little pizzas with any type of toppings you normally prefer on your favorite pizza. Just be sure to put the cheese on first.

3 You will need to use your fingers to sprinkle or layer the toppings! Be sure to preheat the oven so the matzo crackers do not burn.

4 Place 2 crackers on a baking sheet. Bake in 350-degree preheated oven for 15 minutes. Remove pizza with a spatula from the baking sheet to a cutting board. Using a pizza cutter, cut each pizza into 4 squares. Repeat for as many pizzas as you are serving!

PIZZA COMBINATIONS

Bake all combinations as directed in the PREP COACH *above.*

Tomato, Pepperoni and Spinach—For each pizza, sprinkle a cracker with 1/2 cup shredded mozzarella cheese. Top with 2/3 cup spinach leaves, 4 thin slices of fresh tomatoes of medium size, 16 small slices pepperoni and 1/4 cup drained sliced black olives. Sprinkle with a pinch of oregano.

Ground Turkey, Cheddar and Green Chile—Sauté 1/2 pound ground turkey in 1 tablespoon olive oil until cooked through and crumbly. Season to taste with salt, pepper and thyme. For each pizza, sprinkle a cracker with 1/2 cup Cheddar cheese. Top with 1/2 cup of the cooked ground turkey and 3 tablespoons canned, diced green chilies. Sprinkle with a pinch of thyme.

Ham, Swiss and Pineapple—For each pizza, sprinkle each cracker with 1/2 cup shredded Swiss cheese. Top with 1/2 cup cooked diced ham, 1/2 cup diced pineapple that has been drained in a colander and 1 tablespoon canned, diced jalapeño.

Shrimp, Harvarti and Artichoke—Chop 1/2 cup canned artichoke hearts (about 4 of them) and drain them on paper a towel. For each pizza, lay thin slices of Havarti cheese to cover a cracker. Top with 16 very small cooked shrimp (tails removed) and the chopped artichokes. Sprinkle with a pinch of parsley.

Gourmet—For each pizza, spread 3 tablespoons room temperature mascarpone cheese on a cracker. Spread with 2 tablespoons fig jam. Lay fresh arugula leaves on top of the jam. Top with 4 thin slices tomato and 3 to 4 thin slices prosciutto. Sprinkle with a pinch of dried rosemary.

Bruschetta 3 Ways

Makes 20 to 24 pieces

Ingredients

1   cup cannelloni beans, rinsed and
     drained
6   teaspoons olive oil
3   teaspoons white wine vinegar
1   tablespoon minced fresh parsley
Salt and pepper to taste
1   cup finely chopped fresh
     tomatoes
1   green onion, thinly sliced
1   teaspoon finely minced garlic
3/4 cup finely diced green or yellow
     zucchini
1/4 cup finely diced onion
Pinch of oregano
1   long loaf of baguette bread
1/2 cup Parmesan cheese

Preparation

Preheat oven to 300 degrees.

Place the cannelloni beans in a small bowl and add 2 teaspoons oil, 1 teaspoon vinegar and the parsley and stir. Add a pinch of salt and pepper to taste and set aside.

Place the tomatoes and green onion into another small bowl and add 2 teaspoons oil, 1 teaspoon vinegar and the garlic and stir. Add a pinch of salt and pepper to taste and set aside.

In another small bowl, add the zucchini, onion, 2 teaspoons olive oil, 1 teaspoon vinegar and the oregano and stir. Add a pinch of salt and pepper to taste and set aside.

Using a serrated knife, slice the bread into twenty-four 1/2-inch slices.

Lay bread slices in a single layer on a large baking sheet and spray the top side of each with a bit of butter or olive oil spray.

Bake in the oven at 300 degrees for about 6 to 8 minutes until lightly toasted.

Remove baguettes from the oven and leaving them on the baking sheets, top 8 of the slices with cannelloni beans, 8 with the tomatoes and 8 with the zucchini and onion.

Sprinkle a bit of the Parmesan cheese on top of each bruschetta and place under the broiler for a minute or two to melt the cheese.

MOZZARELLA AND ROASTED GARLIC BREAD

Makes 12 to 24 pieces

INGREDIENTS

1   whole head of garlic
1/2 teaspoon olive oil
1   whole loaf of Italian or
    French bread
3   tablespoons room temperature
    butter
1   cup shredded low-moisture
    mozzarella cheese (do not use
    buffalo mozzarella)
2   tablespoons finely chopped
    fresh parsley
1/2 teaspoon salt
1/2 teaspoon pepper
1/4 teaspoon paprika

PREPARATION

Preheat oven to 350 degrees.

To roast the garlic, cut off one end of the whole head of garlic, leaving the papery skin on (garlic cloves can be squeezed from the skin after being roasted).

Place the head of garlic in a bit of foil, drizzle with olive oil. Cover garlic with the foil and bake at 350 degrees for 1 hour.

Remove garlic from the oven and allow it to cool in the foil.

Uncover the garlic and squeeze each clove into a small bowl. Mash with a fork (larger pieces may need to be cut with a knife or scissors).

Slice the loaf of bread lengthwise so you have 2 long pieces.

With a flat knife, spread about 1 1/2 tablespoons butter over each piece of bread, then spread desired amount of roasted garlic over each.

Sprinkle 1/2 cup mozzarella cheese over each.

Evenly sprinkle on the parsley, salt, pepper and paprika.

Set the oven to broil.

Place both slices of garlic bread on a large cookie sheet and broil until the bread is toasted and cheese is bubbly, about 3 to 4 minutes.

Slice the bread into 2-inch pieces and serve on a platter.

Rick's Brat Bites with Mustard Sauce

Serves 12

Ingredients

1/4 cup spicy brown mustard
1/4 cup yellow mustard
1   tablespoon diced onion
1   tablespoon mayonnaise
1/2 teaspoon horseradish
6   bratwurst sausages
6   small tortillas

Preparation

To make the mustard sauce, mix the mustards, onion, mayonnaise and horseradish in a small bowl.

Grill or panfry the sausages to preferred doneness, allow to cool for about 5 minutes, then slice each sausage into 6 pieces.

Slice each tortilla into 6 strips.

Wrap one tortilla strip around each sausage bite and secure with a toothpick.

Serve the brat bites with the sauce for dipping.

Chinese Chicken Wings

Serves 8, about 3 wings per person

Ingredients

1/4 cup soy sauce
1/4 cup teriyaki sauce
1   tablespoon honey
1   tablespoon rice vinegar
1   teaspoon hot chili oil
3   green onions, sliced
1   (2 1/2-pound) bag of frozen unseasoned and uncooked chicken wings (approximately 24 wings)
1/2 teaspoon each celery salt, garlic powder and pepper
1   tablespoon sesame seeds
1   small bag shredded tri-color cabbage and 2 sliced green onions

Preparation

Place the soy, teriyaki, honey, vinegar, hot oil and green onions in a gallon-size sealable plastic bag.

Add the wings to the marinade, then seal and refrigerate for 3 hours turning occasionally.

Drain marinade and place wings skin side down in a 9×13-inch baking dish.

Sprinkle with the celery salt, garlic powder and pepper.

Bake at 425 degrees for 10 minutes. Remove from oven.

Turn the wings over and evenly sprinkle on the sesame seeds. Bake for another 15 to 20 minutes or until browned and cooked through.

If desired, turn the oven to broil to further brown the wings for 2 to 3 minutes.

Serve on a platter in a bed of shredded cabbage and sprinkle sliced fresh green onions over the top.

PORK SKEWERS WITH BBQ AND HOLLANDAISE

Serves 4

INGREDIENTS

1   small bottle of prepared
    hollandaise sauce, or 1 packet of
    hollandaise sauce mix (will need
    only about 1 cup of the sauce)
2   pork loin chops, cut into
    16 (1-inch) pieces
1   red or green bell pepper, cut into
    16 (2-inch) pieces
16 small whole button mushrooms
2   cups of your favorite BBQ sauce
8   small metal skewers, or 8 wood
    skewers soaked in water for
    10 minutes

PREPARATION

Preheat BBQ grill to medium-
    high heat.
Make the hollandaise sauce
    according to package directions.
    (If you prefer to make your own
    sauce, use the Texas Tri-Tip sauce
    on page 44.)
Alternately skewer 2 pieces each of
    the pork, pepper and mushrooms
    onto a skewer; repeat with the
    other 7 skewers.

Brush the pork skewers on all sides
    with the BBQ sauce.
Grill the skewers on one side for
    6 minutes; turn over and grill for
    another 6 minutes or until done.
Place skewers on a clean serving
    platter and drizzle each with
    approximately 2 tablespoons of
    the Hollandaise sauce.

MUSHROOM AND ASIAGO CHEESE DIP

Serves 4 to 6

INGREDIENTS

1   (6-ounce) package button
    mushrooms, sliced thin
1   teaspoon olive oil
1   cup mayonnaise
1   cup sour cream
3/4 cup asiago cheese
1/2 cup sliced green onions
1   loaf of baguette bread, cut into
    1/4-inch slices

PREPARATION

Preheat oven to 350 degrees.
Sauté the mushrooms in the olive oil
    in a small skillet over medium-
    high heat for 6 minutes.
In a small baking dish, add the
    mayonnaise, sour cream, cheese

and green onions and mix well.
    Stir in the mushrooms.
Bake, uncovered, for 35 minutes or
    until bubbly and the top is a light
    golden brown.
Serve with the bread slices.

Gridiron Guacamole

Serves 6 to 8

Ingredients

5   very ripe avocados, pits removed
3   garlic cloves, minced
1   small tomato, finely chopped
1   teaspoon lime juice
2   tablespoons sour cream
1/2 teaspoon onion powder
1   teaspoon seasoned salt
4   dashes of your favorite hot sauce, such as Tabasco sauce

Preparation

In a large shallow bowl, mash avocados with a potato masher, leaving a slightly chunky consistency.

Add all other ingredients and stir well. Serve with tortilla chips or celery stalks.

Can't Get Over the Jalapeño Onion Dip

Serves 6 to 8

Ingredients

16 ounces sour cream
1   envelope dry onion soup mix
1   teaspoon butter
1/2 cup minced yellow onion
1/4 cup finely shredded Cheddar cheese
2   teaspoons finely minced jalapeño (seeds and stems removed)

Preparation

Add the sour cream to a medium bowl and thoroughly stir in the onion soup mix.

Melt the butter in a small skillet over medium heat. Add the onion and sauté until soft and golden, about 5 minutes.

Allow onions to cool, then add them to the bowl of sour cream.

Stir in the Cheddar cheese and jalapeño.

Serve with chips and crackers.

BEEFY BEAN DIP

Serves 6 to 8

INGREDIENTS

1   pound ground beef
1/2 cup diced onion
1   (16-ounce) can refried beans
1   cup salsa
1   cup shredded Colby Longhorn
     cheese

PREPARATION

Cook the ground beef in a medium pot over medium-high heat until crumbly, about 8 minutes. Drain beef in a colander to drain off the fat, if desired.

Place beef back into the pot, add onion and cook for another 2 minutes.

Add the refried beans and stir until beans are softened and incorporated.

Add the salsa and cheese and stir until the cheese has melted.

Transfer dip to a serving bowl and serve with tortilla chips.

CORN AND BELL PEPPER SALSA FRESCA

Serves 6 to 8

INGREDIENTS

2   ears of corn, or 2 cups
     frozen corn
3/4 cup diced mix of red and green
     bell peppers
1/2 cup diced tomato
1/4 cup diced red onion
2   teaspoons minced jalapeño chile

2   tablespoons chopped
     fresh cilantro
2   teaspoons olive oil
1   tablespoon fresh lemon juice
1   teaspoon white wine vinegar
1/2 teaspoon salt
1/2 teaspoon pepper

PREPARATION

If using fresh corn, take an ear of corn, stand it on end, and carefully slice off the kernels (it helps to do this in a wide shallow bowl so the kernels stay contained). Repeat with the other ear of corn.

Mix all ingredients in a small bowl and serve with tortilla chips or celery stalks.

REPORTING FROM THE SIDELINES

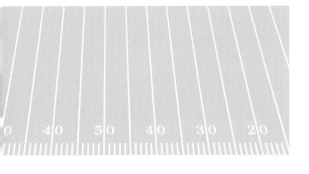

We have named this section of our cookbook in honor of all the smart and talented women who have made their way into the difficult world of football announcing and reporting. From full-on meals such as our Baked Potato Bar, to rich and satisfying sides like the Three Wide Set Mac' and Cheese, to beautiful and healthy salads…these sides are for you! Don't forget to bring one of these delicious sides with you to your next football party!

ULTIMATE TACO SALAD

Serves 6

WARM INGREDIENTS

3/4 pound ground beef
1   large portabello mushroom cap,
    chopped
1   medium onion, chopped
1   celery stalk, chopped
1   large carrot, chopped
1/2 jalapeño pepper, seeds removed
    and minced
1   (15-ounce) can beans (Santé Fe,
    red kidney or garbanzo), drained
    and rinsed
1/2 cup water

SPICES

1   tablespoon chili powder
1   teaspoon garlic powder
1   teaspoon seasoned salt
1/4 teaspoon red pepper
1/4 teaspoon cumin

SALAD INGREDIENTS

1/2 head of iceberg lettuce, cored
    and chopped
1   small can sliced olives
2   medium tomatoes, coarsely
    chopped
4   green onions, sliced
1   avocado, peeled, pitted and
    coarsely chopped
3/4 cup grated Cheddar cheese

PREPARATION

In a large skillet, sauté ground beef
    on medium-high heat until
    cooked through and crumbly.
    Drain fat from ground beef in a
    colander and let rest there.
Wipe most of the fat from the skillet,
    return to medium-high heat
    and add next 5 ingredients
    (mushroom through jalapeño
    pepper). Add spices.
Sauté mushroom and spice mixture
    until browned, approximately
    8 minutes.
Add drained ground beef. Add beans
    and water and stir for 1 minute.
    Reduce heat and simmer for
    10 minutes. Remove from heat
    and allow to cool for about
    5 minutes.
While beef mixture is cooling, add
    lettuce, olives, tomatoes and green
    onions to a large serving bowl.
Add the beef mixture to the lettuce
    (beef and beans should still be
    slightly warm). Thoroughly toss
    to coat.
Add avocado and cheese. Lightly toss
    and serve warm immediately.

SHRIMP AND AVOCADO SALAD

Serves 4 to 6

SALAD INGREDIENTS

2   cups very small precooked
    shrimp, defrosted (peel and
    devein if necessary)
2   avocados, peeled, pitted and
    coarsely chopped
1¹/2 cups hearts of palm, sliced to
    medium thickness
3   green onions, sliced thin
2   celery stalks, diced
2   cloves garlic, minced
3   tablespoons chopped
    fresh parsley

DRESSING INGREDIENTS

2   tablespoons white wine vinegar
1   teaspoon Dijon mustard
¹/4 cup olive oil
¹/4 teaspoon salt
¹/4 teaspoon pepper

PREPARATION

Add shrimp, avocados, hearts of palm,
    green onions, celery, garlic and
    parsley to a medium serving bowl.
For the dressing, add vinegar and
    Dijon mustard to a small bowl
    and whisk to combine.
Slowly add olive oil while you
    vigorously whisk (this should
    thicken the dressing a bit).
Add salt and pepper to taste.
Pour dressing over the shrimp
    mixture and toss.

TRI-COLOR PASTA SALAD

Serves 8 as a side

SALAD INGREDIENTS

8   ounces dried tri-colored
    rotini pasta
1   cup broccoli that has been
    chopped into very small florets
¹/2 cup diced green bell pepper
¹/2 cup diced red bell pepper
¹/4 cup diced red onion
1   cup finely chopped yellow
    squash

DRESSING INGREDIENTS

¹/2 cup beef stock
¹/3 cup olive oil
3   tablespoons red wine vinegar
2   tablespoons fresh chopped
    Italian parsley
1   hard-boiled egg, chopped
¹/2 teaspoon salt
¹/4 teaspoon pepper

PREPARATION

Add pasta to a medium pot and cover
    with water.
Cook according to package directions,
    then drain in a colander and rinse.
Add pasta, broccoli, bell peppers, red
    onion and squash to a large bowl.
To make the dressing, add beef stock,
    oil and vinegar to a small bowl
    and whisk. Stir in parsley and egg.
Pour the dressing over the salad and
    toss well. Add salt and pepper.

ITALIAN ANTIPASTO SALAD

Serves 6 to 8

INGREDIENTS

1   (14-ounce) can artichoke hearts, drained and chopped
1   (14-ounce) can hearts of palm, drained and sliced
1   (14-ounce) can cannelloni beans, drained and rinsed
8   ounces whole canned mushrooms, drained
8   ounces whole black olives, drained
2   cloves garlic, minced
1/2 teaspoon oregano
1/4 cup olive oil
2   tablespoons white wine vinegar
1   teaspoon salt
1/2 teaspoon pepper

PREPARATION

In a large bowl, add the artichokes, hearts of palm, beans, mushrooms, olives, garlic and oregano. Pour in the olive oil and vinegar and toss to coat. Season to taste with salt and pepper.

SWEET BEAN SALAD

Serves 6

INGREDIENTS

1   (15-ounce) can green beans, drained
1   (15-ounce) can yellow wax beans, drained
1   (15-ounce) can kidney beans, drained and rinsed well
1   (15-ounce) can garbanzo beans, drained and rinsed
1/2 cup cider vinegar
1/4 cup sugar
1/4 cup olive oil
1   teaspoon salt
1/2 teaspoon pepper

PREPARATION

Add all 4 cans of beans to a large serving bowl. For the dressing, in a medium bowl, add the vinegar then the sugar and stir until sugar is mostly dissolved. Add the oil, salt and pepper and stir to combine. Pour dressing over the beans and stir well.

Refreshing Cucumber Salad

Serves 6

INGREDIENTS

1/4 cup sugar
1/4 cup cider vinegar
2 cucumbers
8 thin slices of yellow or white onion, each slice cut in half
1 teaspoon (heaping) kosher salt

PREPARATION

In a small bowl, stir the sugar and cider vinegar together until sugar is dissolved.

Peel cucumbers with a potato peeler. Using the slicing side of a box grater or a mandoline, thinly slice the cucumbers and add them to a wide shallow bowl.

Add the onion slices to the bowl of cucumbers.

Add the salt to the cucumbers and onions and stir well.

Pour the sugar-vinegar mixture over and stir well to coat.

Refrigerate for at least 1 hour and up to 3 days.

Potato Salad with Bits of Bacon

Serves 6 to 8

SALAD INGREDIENTS

5 russet potatoes, peeled and cut into 1-inch chunks
2 beef bouillon cubes

2 hard-boiled eggs, sliced
1/3 cup sliced green onion (use both light and dark green parts)

DRESSING INGREDIENTS

1/2 cup mayonnaise
2 tablespoons olive oil
1/4 cup milk
2 tablespoons cider vinegar
1/4 cup crumbled bacon or purchased bacon bits
1/2 teaspoon salt
1/2 teaspoon pepper

PREPARATION

Place potatoes in a large pot and cover with water. Add beef bouillon cubes.

Bring to a boil, reduce heat and simmer for 8 to 10 minutes or until potatoes are cooked to preferred doneness. Drain in a colander and rinse with cold water.

Place potatoes in a serving bowl and allow them to cool for 10 minutes.

For the dressing, whisk ingredients in a small bowl until blended.

Add dressing to the potatoes and toss well. Add more salt and pepper to taste.

Fold in the hard-boiled eggs. Garnish with the green onion.

Buffalo Mozzarella and Tomato Stack

Serves 4

Ingredients

4   vine-ripened or beefsteak tomatoes
1   (12-ounce) piece of buffalo
    mozzarella
12 fresh basil leaves
4   teaspoons olive oil
4   teaspoons balsamic vinegar
8   black or green olives (optional)
Salt and pepper

Preparation

Slice the stem end off of each tomato, and then slice each tomato into 3 slices.

Slice the mozzarella into 12 slices.

Place 1 slice of mozzarella on each of 4 salad plates. Top the mozzarella with 1 tomato slice, then top with 1 basil leaf. Repeat in order to create a "stack" of 3 slices of mozzarella, 3 tomato slices and 3 basil leaves on each plate.

Drizzle 1 teaspoon olive oil and 1 teaspoon vinegar over each stack.

Place 2 olives on each of 4 toothpicks and place on top of each stack as a garnish, if desired. Sprinkle a pinch of salt and pepper over each stack.

Old-Fashioned Iceberg Wedge

Serves 4

Ingredients

1   head of iceberg lettuce

Blue Cheese Dressing

1/2 cup light mayonnaise
1/4 cup sour cream
2   tablespoons olive oil
2   teaspoons honey
1/4 teaspoon Worcestershire sauce
2   teaspoons white wine vinegar
1/3 cup finely crumbled blue cheese
2   tablespoons milk

Preparation

Cut the head of lettuce in half, then cut one of the halves into 4 wedges, leaving out the core. Store the remaining half head of lettuce for future use.

To make the dressing, add the blue cheese dressing ingredients to a small bowl and whisk well.

Place one lettuce wedge on each of 4 salad plates.

Pour desired amount of dressing over each wedge.

MAGGIE'S SPINACH AND STRAWBERRY SALAD

Serves 6

SALAD INGREDIENTS

1   teaspoon butter
1/2 cup slivered almonds
1   pound fresh baby spinach,
    washed and dried
1   pint fresh strawberries, washed,
    hulled and cut in half

DRESSING INGREDIENTS

1/4 cup flaxseed oil plus 1/4 cup
    sunflower oil, or 1/2 cup canola oil
1/4 cup tarragon vinegar
2   tablespoons honey
2   tablespoons sesame seeds
1   tablespoon poppy seeds
1   tablespoon minced white onion
1/4 teaspoon Worcestershire sauce
1/4 teaspoon paprika
Salt and pepper to taste

PREPARATION

Add all dressing ingredients to a
    blender and blend until smooth.
Melt butter in a small skillet and
    sauté almonds for 1 minute or
    until toasted.
Add spinach and strawberries to a
    large serving bowl.
Pour desired amount of dressing over
    the salad and toss.
Garnish with the almonds.

MUSHROOM RISOTTO

Serves 4 to 6

INGREDIENTS

4   cups hot chicken broth
1   tablespoon butter
6   ounces fresh mushrooms,
    chopped (we prefer shiitake
    or cremini)
1/2 cup green onions, sliced thin,
    both light and dark green parts,
    (approximately 3 onions)
2   cloves garlic, minced
1/4 teaspoon dried thyme
1 1/2 cups arborio rice
1/2 cup white wine
3/4 cup grated Parmesan cheese

PREPARATION

Place chicken broth in a 5- or 6-quart
    pot and bring to a simmer.
    Reduce heat and keep the broth
    warm but not boiling throughout
    the risotto-making process.
Heat butter in a medium-size pot
    over medium heat until melted.
Add mushrooms, green onions, garlic
    and thyme and sauté for 1 minute.
Add rice and continue sautéing for
    3 more minutes.
Add wine and cook until evaporated.

Using a ladle, add the hot chicken
    broth in 1-ladle increments. Wait
    to add each ladle of broth until
    previous liquid has evaporated,
    stirring frequently. This process
    takes about 25 minutes.
You may not need all of the broth, so
    taste for doneness prior to using
    it all. Risotto should be slightly
    al dente.
When done, remove from heat. Allow
    to cool for 1 or 2 minutes.
Stir in Parmesan cheese.

Third Down and Dirty Rice

Serves 8 to 10

For a Cajun style of dirty rice, the rice is boiled in advance and then added to other ingredients after they have been sautéed. As a main dish, dirty rice is usually cooked with some type of ground meat or chopped chicken livers to give it the "dirty" appearance. As a side dish, we leave out the meat and sauté a nice mix of Cajun-style veggies. This recipe is featured with Gary's Louisiana Gumbo on page 36, which feeds eight. Halve this recipe for fewer folks!

Ingredients

3 cups uncooked plain white rice (will yield about 9 to 10 cups cooked rice)
3 beef bouillon cubes
4 tablespoons butter
1 cup diced onion
1 cup diced green pepper
1 cup diced celery
2 cloves garlic, minced
1 cup diced tomatoes
1/2 teaspoon salt
1/4 teaspoon cayenne pepper

Preparation

Cook rice according to package directions, adding the bouillon cubes to the water for added salt and flavor.

While rice is cooking, melt 2 tablespoons of the butter in a large pot over medium-high heat (large enough so that the rice can be added later).

Add onion, green pepper and celery. Sauté until soft, about 6 minutes. Add garlic and sauté for 1 minute.

Reduce heat to medium-low and add the cooked rice and remaining 2 tablespoons butter and stir to combine, sautéing for about 3 minutes. Add tomatoes, salt and cayenne pepper. Stir and cook for 1 or 2 minutes.

Sesame Jasmine Rice

Serves 4

Ingredients

2 cups beef broth
1 cup jasmine rice
1 teaspoon sesame oil
1/4 cup diced carrot
1/4 cup diced celery
1/4 cup sliced green onion

Preparation

In a medium pot, bring beef broth and sesame oil to a boil.

Add rice, bring to a boil; reduce to a simmer then cover and simmer 5 minutes.

Add carrot, celery and green onion; cover and simmer another 10 minutes.

Remove from heat; uncover, stir and allow to sit for 5 minutes.

THREE WIDE SET MAC' AND CHEESE

Serves 4

INGREDIENTS

3   tablespoons butter
3   tablespoons flour
2   cups plus 2 tablespoons milk
1   beef bouillon cube
1/2   cup shredded yellow Cheddar
      cheese
1/2   cup white Cheddar cheese
1/2   cup asiago cheese
1   (4-ounce) can diced green chilies
      (optional)
2   cups elbow macaroni
1/4   cup bread crumbs

PREPARATION

Melt the butter over medium heat.
Add flour and whisk until smooth
    (about 1 minute).
Add 2 cups milk and whisk again until
    smooth. Add the bouillon cube.
Increase heat to high and whisking
    constantly, bring sauce to a boil.
Reduce heat and allow sauce to
    simmer until the bouillon cube
    is dissolved and sauce thickens,
    whisking for about 3 minutes more.
Remove from heat and immediately
    add yellow Cheddar cheese,
    white Cheddar cheese and asiago
    cheese. Whisk until cheese melts.

Whisk in 2 more tablespoons milk to
    thin the sauce a bit, if desired.
Optionally add diced green chilies for
    a bit of a kick.
You may keep the cheese sauce warm
    on very low heat, but do not
    allow it boil.
Boil 2 cups elbow macaroni in 5 cups
    water. Cook according to package
    directions. Drain macaroni and
    place in a 2-quart baking dish.
    Add cheese sauce and stir.
Top with bread crumbs and bake,
    covered, at 350 degrees for
    25 minutes.

ASPARAGUS WITH GRAPE TOMATOES AND ROMANO CHEESE

Serves 2

INGREDIENTS

2   teaspoons olive oil
12   asparagus spears
1/2   teaspoon each salt and pepper
6   grape tomatoes, each sliced
      in half
2   tablespoons grated Romano
      cheese

PREPARATION

Heat olive oil in a medium skillet
    over medium high heat.
Add asparagus, salt and pepper and
    sauté for about 5 minutes or
    until close to preferred doneness.

Add the tomatoes and sauté until
    tomatoes are a bit softened,
    about 1 minute.
Divide asparagus and tomatoes
    between dinner plates and
    sprinkle with Romano cheese.

Vagabond Veggies (A Super Succotash)

Serves 6

Ingredients

2   ears of fresh corn on the cob
1   tablespoon butter
3/4 cup diced red bell pepper
1   cup diced onion
1   cup (2-inch pieces) green beans
1   cup green zucchini, sliced into
    1/4-inch rounds, each round
    halved then halved again

1   cup yellow zucchini, sliced into
    1/4-inch rounds, each round
    halved then halved again
2   cloves garlic, minced
1   teaspoon celery salt
1/2 teaspoon black pepper
1/4 teaspoon crushed red pepper or
    cayenne pepper

Preparation

Stand corn on end one ear at a time, and carefully slice off the kernels into a wide shallow bowl.

Melt butter in a large skillet over medium heat.

Add bell pepper and onion and sauté for 2 minutes. Add green beans and sauté for 2 minutes. Add zucchini and sauté for 2 minutes. Add corn, garlic, celery salt, black pepper and red pepper and sauté for another 2 minutes.

Green Beans with Feta Cheese

Serves 4

Ingredients

1   pound green beans, trimmed and
    cut into 3-inch pieces
1/3 cup olive oil
3   tablespoons white wine vinegar
1/2 teaspoon dried dill
1/4 teaspoon each salt and pepper
6   thin slices red onion, each slice
    cut in half
1/2 cup crumbled feta cheese

Preparation

Add green beans to a medium pot and cover with water. Over high heat, bring beans to a boil; reduce heat and simmer for 6 minutes.

For the dressing, in a small bowl, mix the oil, vinegar, dill, salt and pepper.

Drain the beans and add them to a medium serving bowl.

Pour desired amount of dressing over the beans (beans can be either warm or chilled).

Add red onion and feta cheese and lightly toss.

Carolina-Style Pork and Beans

Serves 8 as a side

Ingredients

1   teaspoon olive oil
1   onion, finely chopped
2   garlic cloves, minced
2   (15-ounce) cans of your favorite
    pork and beans
1/4 cup ketchup
1   tablespoon brown sugar
1   tablespoon spicy brown mustard
1   tablespoon cider vinegar
1/4 teaspoon pepper

Preparation

Heat the olive oil in a medium pot; add the onion and sauté until soft, about 5 minutes.
Add the garlic and sauté another minute.

Add the beans, ketchup, brown sugar, mustard, vinegar and pepper.
Stir, bring to a boil; reduce to simmer and simmer 15 to 20 minutes.

Broccoli with Almond Browned Butter

Serves 6

Ingredients

6   cups (2-inch pieces) broccoli
1/2 teaspoon salt
3   tablespoons butter
3/4 cup slivered almonds
    (or 1 (2 1/4-ounce) package)

Preparation

Add broccoli and salt to a medium pot and cover with water. Bring to a boil and once at boiling, cook for 3 to 4 minutes or to preferred doneness.
While broccoli is cooking, melt butter in a small skillet over medium-low to medium heat.
Once melted, allow butter to cook for about 2 minutes until browned, swirling frequently (butter will foam and bubble a bit).

Add almonds (butter will continue to foam) and immediately remove from heat.
Stir the almonds, allowing the almond browned butter to cool for about 3 minutes (as the mixture cools, the almonds will turn golden brown).
Drain broccoli, place in a serving bowl and toss with the almond browned butter.

BRUSSELS SPROUTS WITH SHALLOT CREAM

Serves 4

INGREDIENTS

2   tablespoons butter
16 brussels sprouts (or 4 per
    person), stems trimmed and
    cut in half
1/2 cup diced shallots
1/2 cup half-and-half
1/4 teaspoon salt
1/4 teaspoon pepper
1/4 teaspoon thyme

PREPARATION

Melt butter in a large skillet over medium-high heat (skillet should be fitted with a lid). Add brussels sprouts and sauté until soft but still firm, about 5 minutes (some of the leaves will fall off; this is okay.). Add shallots and sauté 1 minute.

Add half-and-half, salt, pepper and thyme. Immediately reduce heat and stir until cream is at a simmer. Cover and simmer until brussels sprouts are cooked through and tender, stirring occasionally, about 5 to 6 minutes.

CHEESY CAULIFLOWER

Serves 4 to 6

INGREDIENTS

3   tablespoons butter
3   tablespoons flour
2   cups plus 2 tablespoons milk
1   beef bouillon cube
1   cup shredded yellow
    Cheddar cheese
4   cups (2-inch) cauliflower florets
1/2 teaspoon salt

PREPARATION

Melt butter over low heat. Add flour and whisk until smooth (about 1 minute).

Add 2 cups milk and whisk again until smooth. Add the bouillon cube. Increase heat to high and whisking constantly, bring sauce to a boil.

Reduce heat and allow sauce to simmer until the bouillon cube is dissolved and sauce thickens, whisking occasionally for about 3 minutes more.

Remove from heat and immediately add Cheddar cheese. Whisk until cheese melts. Whisk in 2 more tablespoons milk to thin the sauce, if desired. You may keep the sauce warm on very low heat, but do not allow it to boil.

Place cauliflower in a medium pot and cover with water. Add salt.

Bring cauliflower to a boil over high heat. Reduce heat and simmer for 3 to 4 minutes. Drain cauliflower in a colander and place in a serving bowl.

Add cheese sauce and stir gently.

Sugar Snap Peas with a Cashew Crunch

Serves 4

Ingredients

2   teaspoons olive oil
3/4 pound whole sugar snap peas
1/2 cup cashews
1   tablespoon sesame seeds
1   tablespoon soy sauce
1/4 teaspoon salt
1/4 teaspoon pepper
1/4 teaspoon ginger powder

Preparation

Heat olive oil in a medium skillet over medium-high heat. Add sugar snap peas and sauté until slightly soft but still firm, about 5 minutes.

Add cashews and sesame seeds and sauté for another minute.

Add soy sauce, salt, pepper and ginger and sauté for another minute or two until peas are tender.

Creamy Mashed Potatoes

Serves 6

Ingredients

3   large russet potatoes, peeled and chopped into 1-inch pieces
2   beef bouillon cubes (optional)
3   tablespoons butter
3/4 cup cream or half-and-half
1/2 teaspoon salt
1/4 teaspoon pepper

Preparation

Place potatoes in a medium pot and cover completely with water.

Add 2 beef bullion cubes to the water (optional).

Bring to a boil, reduce heat and cook potatoes at a low boil for 15 to 20 minutes or until very soft.

Drain and bring potatoes back to the same pot. Turn off heat.

Add butter, cream, salt and pepper and mash potatoes well to desired consistency.

BAKED POTATO BAR

Serves variable amount

PREP COACH

1 To coat baking potatoes in oil, pour about 2 tablespoons olive oil in a small bowl. Dip your fingers into the bowl as needed to fully coat each potato in oil with your hands. This will ensure a nice crispy skin after baking. Just don't try to catch any footballs afterward!

2 Place potatoes on a baking sheet. This will prevent the salt from spilling all over your oven.

3 Prick each potato with a fork and rub all over with salt. It is best to use sea salt or kosher salt.

PREPARATION

Preheat oven to 350 degrees

Scrub desired number of large russet potatoes (usually 1 per person).

Prepare potatoes according to PREP COACH.

Bake on the baking sheet for 35 minutes. Turn each potato and bake another 35 minutes or to desired doneness.

While potatoes are baking, add the toppings to individual bowls and set out for serving. When the potatoes are ready, cut them open and pile on the toppings in your order of preference!

TOPPINGS

Butter
Sour cream
Chopped green onions
Bacon bits
Shredded Cheddar cheese
Salsa

NEW POTATOES WITH BROWN SUGAR GLAZE

Serves 8, two potatoes each

This recipe is featured with our Mighty Missouri BBQ Ribs on page 30, which feeds eight to ten. Halve this recipe for fewer folks!

INGREDIENTS

16 *small white new potatoes (each potato should be about 3 inches round)*

2 *chicken bouillon cubes*

4 *tablespoons butter*

2 *tablespoons (heaping) brown sugar*

1 *teaspoon salt*

1/2 *teaspoon pepper*

PREPARATION

Add potatoes to a large pot and cover with water. Add bouillon cubes.

Bring to a boil and boil potatoes until tender, about 20 minutes. Drain potatoes. Return to the pot.

Over low heat, add the butter and brown sugar to the potatoes and gently stir to coat, about 1 to 2 minutes. Add salt and pepper.

Soy-Roasted Potatoes and Carrots

Serves 8

Ingredients

4   medium-size russet or red potatoes with skins on, cut into 2-inch pieces
1   (1-pound) package of peeled and trimmed baby carrots (in 2-inch pieces)
3   tablespoons olive oil
1/2   cup soy sauce
1/2   teaspoon dried rosemary
1/2   teaspoon garlic salt
1/2   teaspoon celery salt
1/2   teaspoon pepper

This recipe is featured with our Cleveland Apple- and Portabello-Stuffed Pork Roast on page 26, which feeds eight. Halve this recipe for fewer folks!

Preparation

Preheat oven to 350 degrees.
Add potatoes and carrots to a 9×13-inch baking dish.
Add olive oil and soy sauce. Sprinkle rosemary, garlic salt, celery salt and pepper over the dish. Stir well to coat the potatoes and carrots, and cover with aluminum foil.

Bake for 40 minutes. Remove from oven, uncover and stir well.
Roast for another 20 minutes uncovered. Remove from oven and stir again.
Roast for another 15 minutes or until desired softness.
Stir and place in a large serving bowl.

Blue Cheese-Broiled Tomatoes

Serves 4 with 1 tomato per person, or 8 with 1/2 tomato per person

Ingredients

4   large ripe beefsteak tomatoes
1   tablespoon melted butter
1/2   teaspoon salt
1/2   teaspoon pepper
4   tablespoons (heaping) crumbled blue cheese

Preparation

Preheat oven to 350 degrees.
Slice a very small piece off each end of each tomato so when cut in half, the tomatoes will sit upright on a baking sheet. Cut each tomato in half horizontally.
Place tomatoes (small cut side down) on a rimmed baking sheet and evenly drizzle the melted butter over them.

Sprinkle with the salt and pepper.
Sprinkle a generous 1/2 tablespoon of blue cheese on top of each tomato half.
Bake tomatoes on the center rack for 15 to 20 minutes, then turn on the broiler, leaving them on the center rack for about 2 minutes or until golden on top.

FIVE-RING PINEAPPLE UPSIDE DOWN CAKE

10

FANTASY DESSERTS
& TEAM SPIRITS

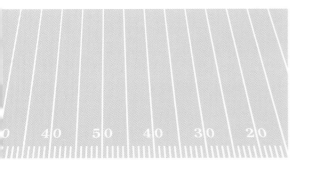

We don't know what you fantasize about after the football game is over, but we fantasize about Grandma...her desserts, of course! Grandma's desserts and cakes were the highlight of every Sunday! She brought most of her recipes to America straight off the boat from Denmark, and we are happy to share a few of them with you translated from pieces of paper and notecards that must be 100 years old or more. Fantasy Desserts? You betcha!

Five-Ring Pineapple Upside-Down Cake

Serves 8

Ingredients

1   (8-ounce) can sliced pineapple
3   tablespoons butter
1/2 cup packed brown sugar
4   maraschino cherries,
     cut into halves
1   cup sifted all-purpose flour
11/4 teaspoons baking powder
1/4 teaspoon salt
1/2 cup granulated sugar
1/3 cup safflower oil
1   egg
1   teaspoon vanilla extract

Preparation

Preheat the oven to 350 degrees.
Drain the pineapple, reserving
     the syrup.
Melt the butter in an 8×8-inch
     baking dish. Stir in the brown
     sugar and 1 tablespoon of the
     reserved syrup.
Arrange the pineapple in the
     prepared baking dish. Place a
     cherry half in the center of each
     ring cut side up.
Sift the flour, baking powder and
     salt together.
Add enough water to the remaining
     pineapple syrup to measure
     1/2 cup.

Beat the sugar and safflower oil in a
     mixing bowl until light.
Add the egg and vanilla and beat
     until fluffy.
Add the flour mixture and pineapple
     syrup mixture alternately, beating
     well after each addition.
Spread over the prepared pineapple
     layer.
Bake for 40 to 45 minutes or until
     golden brown. Cool in the dish
     for 5 minutes and invert onto a
     serving plate. Serve warm.

FRESH BERRY SOUR CREAM COFFEE CAKE

Makes 16 slices

CAKE INGREDIENTS

1   cup sugar
1/2 cup room temperature butter
2   eggs
1/2 teaspoon vanilla
2   cups sour cream
1   cup fresh berries, such as
    raspberries, blueberries or
    blackberries

SIFTED INGREDIENTS

2   cups flour
1   teaspoon baking powder
1   teaspoon baking soda

TOPPING INGREDIENTS

1/4 cup sugar
1/2 teaspoon cinnamon
1/2 cup sliced almonds

PREPARATION

Add the sugar and butter to a mixing bowl and beat to cream the mixture, about 2 minutes. Add eggs and vanilla and beat for another minute.

Add sifted ingredients and beat for another minute or two until also creamed.

Add sour cream and beat for another minute. Gently stir in berries.

In a small bowl, mix together the topping ingredients.

Spray an angel food cake pan with cooking spray.

Spread half of the mixed batter into the bottom of an angel food cake pan.

Sprinkle half the topping ingredients over the batter.

Evenly spread the remaining batter to the cake pan and sprinkle the remaining toppings over the top.

Bake at 350 degrees for 35 minutes.

Remove from oven and allow to cool. Place a plate over the cake pan and invert to plate.

Slice to serve.

GRANDMA'S BANANA NUT BREAD

Makes 12 slices

INGREDIENTS

3/4 cup room temperature margarine
1 1/2 cups sugar
2 eggs
1/2 cup milk
1 tablespoon white vinegar
1/2 teaspoon vanilla
2 cups flour
1 teaspoon baking soda
1/4 teaspoon salt
3 bananas, thinly sliced
1/2 cup walnuts

PREPARATION

Preheat oven to 350 degrees.
Add the margarine and sugar to a mixing bowl and beat to cream the mixture, about 2 minutes. Add the eggs and beat for another minute.
Combine the milk and vinegar in a small bowl and stir.
Add the milk mixture, vanilla, flour, soda and salt and beat for another minute or two.

Add the bananas and beat until the bananas are mostly incorporated, about 1 more minute. Stir in walnuts.
Coat a 9×5-inch bread pan with cooking spray.
Pour batter into pan and bake for 1 hour.
Allow to cool, remove to a plate with a spatula, and slice to serve.

SUGAR-GLAZED LEMON BREAD

Makes 12 slices

INGREDIENTS

1/2 cup each vegetable oil and milk
1 1/2 cups flour
1 cup sugar
1 tablespoon fresh lemon juice
1 teaspoon salt
2 eggs
1 teaspoon baking powder
1/2 cup walnuts (optional)
1/2 cup sugar
1 tablespoon fresh lemon juice

PREPARATION

Preheat oven to 350 degrees.
Add the oil, milk, flour and sugar to a mixing bowl and mix for 2 minutes.
Add 1 tablespoon lemon juice, the salt, eggs and baking powder and mix for another minute. Stir in the walnuts.
Coat a 4 1/2×8 1/2-inch bread pan with cooking spray and sprinkle some flour into it as well.

Pour the batter into the bread pan and bake for 1 hour. Allow to cool in the pan.
Add the sugar to a small bowl. Add 1 tablespoon lemon juice and stir constantly for a minute or so until the sugar becomes a glaze.
Pour the glaze over the lemon bread. When glaze has been absorbed, remove bread from pan and slice to serve.

Brownies with a Cream Cheese Swirl

Makes 9 squares

Swirl Ingredients

3 ounces room temperature
cream cheese
2 tablespoons room temperature
butter
2 tablespoons sugar
1 egg
1/4 teaspoon vanilla
2 tablespoons flour

Swirl Preparation

In another mixing bowl, add all
cream cheese ingredients and
with clean beaters beat until
smooth, about 1 to 2 minutes.

Brownie Ingredients

1/3 cup room temperature butter
3 ounces (3 squares) semisweet
chocolate
1 cup sugar
1/4 teaspoon vanilla

2 eggs
1/2 cup flour
1/4 teaspoon baking powder
1/4 teaspoon salt

Brownie Preparation

Preheat oven to 350 degrees.
In a small pan over low heat, melt
the butter and chocolate squares,
stirring frequently.
When melted, add chocolate to a
mixing bowl; add sugar and beat
for 1 minute. Add vanilla, eggs,
flour, baking powder and salt and
beat for 1 to 2 minutes or until
thick and creamy.
Spray a 9×9-inch baking dish with
cooking spray.

Layer the chocolate mixture and swirl
mixture 1/3 at a time, beginning
with the chocolate. Do not stir
between layers.
With a spatula, gently swirl the
mixture to create a marbling
effect; do not overstir.
Bake at 350 degrees for 25 to
30 minutes.
Allow to cool and then place in the
refrigerator to harden for 2 hours
or overnight.

CHOCOLATE CHIP OATMEAL COOKIES

Makes 32 cookies

INGREDIENTS

1   cup room temperature margarine
3/4 cup each sugar and brown sugar
1   teaspoon vanilla
2   eggs
1   teaspoon hot water
1 1/2 cups flour
1   teaspoon salt
1   teaspoon baking soda
1/2 cup walnuts
1   cup (6 ounces) chocolate chips
2   cups quick-cooking oats

PREPARATION

In a mixing bowl, add margarine, sugar and brown sugar and beat to cream the mixture, about 2 minutes. Add vanilla and 1 egg beat again for 30 seconds. Add the other egg and beat for another 30 seconds or so.

Stir in the hot water. Add flour, salt and soda and beat until just incorporated (do not overmix). Stir in nuts, chips and oats (mixture will be very thick).

Coat a cookie sheet with cooking spray.

Drop 1-inch round cookies onto cookie sheet and bake for about 8 minutes per batch.

BANANA-PINEAPPLE WHIPPED CREAM BARS

Makes 12 squares

INGREDIENTS

1   cup butter
3   cups graham cracker crumbs
1/4 cup chopped walnuts (optional)
2   (8-ounce) packages room temperature cream cheese
2   cups sugar
4   bananas
2   cups crushed pineapple, drained well and patted dry
1   (8-ounce) carton frozen whipped cream, thawed in refrigerator for 5 hours or more

PREPARATION

Melt butter in a pan over low heat. Add the graham crumbs and walnuts to a medium bowl. Pour butter over the crumbs and stir until crumbs are softened and moist. Add all of the crust to an ungreased 9×13-inch glass baking dish. Press crust evenly on the bottom and a bit up the sides of the baking dish.

Place cream cheese and sugar in a mixing bowl and beat until smooth, about 3 to 5 minutes.

Spoon the cream cheese mixture evenly over the crust in large dollops.

Very gently spread the cream cheese over the crust (the crust will come up a bit if you press too hard).

Thinly slice the bananas and lay them evenly over the cream cheese.

Layer the pineapple over the bananas.

Spread whipped cream over the bananas.

Refrigerate about 3 hours to harden before serving.

LATE MORNING HAIL MARYS

Serves variable amount

Bloody Marys are best served help-yourself-style! Here we share some ideas for setting out the ingredients and garnishes on a table for you and your guests to have all sorts of football fun with. We love these cocktails paired with our Bloody Viking BLTs on page 86.

INGREDIENTS

Set the following list of ingredients out on a long table:
A bucket of ice cubes
One or two bottles of good vodka
A couple of shot glasses to measure the vodka with
A pitcher of your favorite tomato juice, vegetable juice or Bloody Mary mix
A bottle of Worcestershire sauce
Bottles of your favorite hot sauces (such as Tabasco)
A shaker of black pepper
A bowl of lemons and limes, cut into wedges
A tall container of whole washed celery sticks (one per person)
Tall drinking glasses

GARNISHES

Add these additional garnishes to your table along with serving forks so you and your guests can pick and choose, and drop them right in the glass.
1   jar of green olives (any kind: pimento-stuffed, jalapeño-stuffed, blue cheese-stuffed, etc.)
1   jar of sweet gherkin pickles
1   jar of kosher dill pickles
1   jar of baby corn
1   jar of prepared horseradish
1   jar of pearl onions
1   jar of marinated mushrooms

PREPARATION

Fill 1 tall drinking glass ¾ full with ice cubes. Add 1 shot of vodka. Fill glass ¾ full with tomato juice or Bloody Mary mix. Add 2 shakes Worcestershire sauce. Add 3 shakes hot sauce. Add a couple shakes of black pepper. Squeeze and add lemon or lime wedge. Add celery stick and stir to combine drink. Add garnishes as desired. Repeat!

PAULA'S MARGARITAS

Serves 4

Our margarita recipe comes from my sister who has only 2 faults: she's a gin drinker and a Cowboys fan. She has been known to make this wonderful 'rita recipe with… you guessed it… gin instead of the tequila. Please do not do this.

INGREDIENTS

Ice
1 (6-ounce) can frozen limeade
4 ounces tequila
2 ounces Triple Sec
1 ounce Grand Mariner or Cointreau
6 ounces beer (Corona works well)
Fresh limes

PREPARATION

Fill a blender halfway with ice. Add the remaining ingredients and blend. Serve in margarita glasses rimmed with salt and a slice of lime.

The easiest way to rim a glass is to sprinkle a generous amount of salt on a plate. Cut a thin slice of lime and rub it around the rim of a margarita glass. Turn the glass upside down and press onto the plate of salt. Fill glass and serve with the slice of lime placed either on the rim or in the glass.

MIKE'S HAIR-OF-THE-DOG MEXICAN MARTINI

Makes 4 (4-ounce) martinis

While visiting Napa one fall, we obtained this martini recipe from a gentleman named Mike Hair that we sat next to during one of the fabulous wine tastings. Thank you, Mike, for the tasty cocktail idea and nice conversation!

INGREDIENTS

3 ounces tequila
1 1/2 ounces Cointreau
6 ounces of your favorite margarita mix (or if you like them less sweet, just use water)
1/2 ounce fresh lime juice
A splash of sweet-and-sour mix
1 jalapeño-stuffed olive along with 1 teaspoon of the olive juice

PREPARATION

Fill a shaker halfway with ice. Add the tequila, Cointreau, margarita mix, lime juice and sweet-and-sour mix.

Shake; strain and serve in a martini glass.

Garnish the glass with sliced lime and one of the olives.

PEACH-FACED LOVEBIRD

Makes 1 lovebird

Wild parrots called peach-faced lovebirds can be seen all over Phoenix, Arizona. We named these drinks after the cute little creatures that love to loudly squawk and play in our backyard.

INGREDIENTS

3 ounces dry white Champagne
1 ounce orange juice
1/2 ounce white rum
1/2 ounce peach liquor

PREPARATION

Add all ingredients to a Champagne glass.

KENNY'S WINTER WARMER

Makes 1 winter warmer

A family tradition while decorating the Christmas tree every year!

INGREDIENTS

1 egg
1 1/2 cups sugar
1 teaspoon allspice
1 teaspoon vanilla
1 cup boiling water
Rum or brandy

PREPARATION

Place the egg and sugar into a small bowl and beat very well with a fork or an electric mixer.

Add the allspice and vanilla and stir well.

Place 1 cup boiling water into a heavy mug.

Add 1 shot of rum or brandy to the mug and top with 2 to 3 tablespoons of the sugar-spice mixture and stir.

The sugar-spice mixture serves about 8 mugs.

If you are concerned about using raw eggs, use eggs pasteurized in their shells, or use an equivalent amount of egg substitute.

INDEX

To order additional copies of

YOUR GRIDIRON GOURMET

A COLLECTION OF RECIPES CELEBRATING
FOOD, FAMILY, FRIENDS, AND FOOTBALL

visit www.yourgridirongourmet.com